PHILIP ALLAN

LITERATURE GUIDE

FOR A-LEVEL

FRANKENSTEIN

MARY SHELLEY

Andrew Green

Series editor: Nicola Onyett

Philip Allan Updates, an imprint of Hodder Education, an Hachette UK company,
Market Place, Deddington, Oxfordshire OX15 0SE

Orders

Bookpoint Ltd, 130 Milton Park, Abingdon, Oxfordshire OX14 4SB
tel: 01235 827827
fax: 01235 400401
e-mail: education@bookpoint.co.uk
Lines are open 9.00 a.m.–5.00 p.m., Monday to Saturday, with a 24-hour message
answering service. You can also order through the Philip Allan Updates website:
www.philipallan.co.uk

ISBN 978-1-4441-1624-3

First printed 2010

Impression number 5 4 3 2 1

Year 2014 2013 2012 2011 2010

Printed in Spain

Hachette UK's policy is to use papers that are natural, renewable and recyclable products
and made from wood grown in sustainable forests. The logging and manufacturing
processes are expected to conform to the environmental regulations of the country of
origin.

Cover photo: © Jeffrey Collingwood/Fotolia

P01729

Contents

Using this guide

Why read this guide?

The purposes of this A-level Literature Guide are to enable you to organise your thoughts and responses to the text, deepen your understanding of key features and aspects and help you to address the particular requirements of examination questions and coursework tasks in order to obtain the best possible grade. It will also prove useful to those of you writing a coursework piece on the text as it provides a number of summaries, lists, analyses and references to help with the content and construction of the assignment.

Note that teachers and examiners are seeking above all else evidence of an *informed personal response to the text*. A guide such as this can help you to understand the text and form your own opinions, and it can suggest areas to think about, but it cannot replace your own ideas and responses as an informed and autonomous reader.

Page references in this guide refer to the 2003 Penguin Classics edition of the text. Where authors' names are cited after quotations, full references are given in the *Taking it further* section on pp. 89–92 of this guide.

How to make the most of this guide

You may find it useful to read sections of this guide when you need them, rather than reading it from start to finish. For example, you may find it helpful to read the *Contexts* section before you start reading the text, or to read the *Chapter summaries and commentaries* section in conjunction with the text — whether to back up your first reading of it at school or college or to help you revise. The sections relating to the Assessment Objectives will be especially useful in the weeks leading up to the exam.

Key elements

Look at the **Context** boxes to find interesting facts that are relevant to the text.

Context

Be exam-ready

Broaden your thinking about the text by answering the questions in the **Pause for thought** boxes. These help you to consider your own opinions in order to develop your skills of criticism and analysis.

*Pause for **Thought***

Build critical skills

Taking it further boxes suggest poems, films, etc. that provide further background or illuminating parallels to the text.

Taking it **Further** ▶

Where to find out more

Use the **Task boxes** to develop your understanding of the text and test your knowledge of it. Answers for some of the tasks are given online, and do not forget to look online for further self-tests on the text.

Task

Test yourself

Follow up cross references to the **Top ten quotations** (see pp. 87–89), where each quotation is accompanied by a commentary that shows why it is important.

❮ Top ten *quotation*

Know your text

Don't forget to go online: **www.philipallan.co.uk/literatureguidesonline** where you can find additional exam responses, a glossary of literary terms, interactive questions, podcasts and much more.

Synopsis

Frankenstein is a classic tale which permeates our culture at many levels. It tells the story of a man-made monster seeking acceptance by society, but finding his efforts hampered at every turn by human prejudice arising from his hideous appearance. Tragically faced by rejection at every turn, the monster exacts his terrible revenge on his creator. Set against the backdrop of 1790s Europe, an era of great social and political ferment, the story explores the nature of prejudice and issues of profound personal, social and moral significance. It begins with a series of letters exchanged between Captain Robert Walton and his sister that chronicle the story of a man, Victor Frankenstein, whom he meets on a journey in the Northern ocean when Walton's ship is caught in ice.

Rescued from death, Frankenstein gives Walton the account of his upbringing and his early fascination with understanding how to create life. While studying at Ingolstadt, he becomes an obsessive amateur scientist seeking to create a 'perfect' human from body parts exhumed from graves. His plan backfires and his creature turns out to be monstrously ugly, which Frankenstein wrongly takes as a reflection of his creature's personality. He shamelessly abandons his creation. Frankenstein breaks down but is nursed by his friend Clerval.

On the eve of returning to Geneva, Frankenstein learns that his youngest brother, William, has been murdered. As he approaches home, Frankenstein sees the monster and realises at once that he is the murderer. Frankenstein decides not to disclose this, convincing himself that everyone will simply dismiss him as insane. When he reaches his home, he learns that Justine Moritz, a close family friend, has been accused of the murder. Still Frankenstein does not intervene, and Justine is tried and executed. Frankenstein is forced to face up to reality; he wanders in the mountains, where the monster seeks him out and confronts him with the pitiful story of his life.

After leaving Frankenstein's laboratory, he sought companionship, but received only insults and abuse wherever he went. Eventually he found refuge in a hovel next to a small house inhabited by an old, blind man and his two children. As he watches the family and reads their books, the monster learns to speak and read. He has a good nature and feels compassion for the struggling family, and helps them out in secret. He longs to be part of this kind and protective unit, and contrives to meet them. He first speaks with the blind man, but when his children return they are horrified and beat the monster, so he flees. The monster is completely disillusioned and burns with rage. He sets out to find Frankenstein to demand that he fulfils his responsibilities as his creator, but by chance comes across Frankenstein's brother in the forest. Overcome with the desire for revenge, he strangles the boy and incriminates the hapless Justine Moritz by hiding the boy's locket on her.

Having told his story, the monster requests that Frankenstein should create another being: a female to be his companion. He promises Frankenstein that if he complies, the monster and his bride will live in seclusion, far from the humans who have treated him so badly. The monster is measured and rational, and convinces Frankenstein there is justice in his claims. Frankenstein also feels for the first time that he has a duty towards the creature he has brought into the world, although also to his fellow man. He reluctantly agrees to the monster's request and leaves for England to complete his work, accompanied by Clerval. On his return, he plans to marry Elizabeth.

Once engaged in work on his second creation, he begins to have second thoughts. He worries that the creatures may not like each other, or that they may breed, begetting a whole race of monsters. When the monster visits to make sure Frankenstein is as good as his word, Frankenstein destroys the second creature. The monster vows vengeance and promises to be with Frankenstein on his wedding night. The following day a body is found and Frankenstein is accused of murder. Taken to see the corpse, he discovers that the dead man is Clerval. Eventually, after a long illness, Frankenstein is cleared of murder and returns to Geneva, where he marries Elizabeth, promising to tell her his horrifying secrets. Frankenstein is convinced that the monster intends to kill him that night, but the monster kills Elizabeth instead. Frankenstein's father dies of shock and Frankenstein now loses every desire except for revenge. He chases the monster to and fro across Europe, eventually finding himself in the Arctic, where he encounters Walton.

Once he has finished his tale, the dying Frankenstein asks Walton to pursue the monster and to kill him on his behalf if he dies before he can do it himself. The ship breaks free of the ice and Walton, under pressure from his crew, decides to abandon his trip and return home. Frankenstein dies and Walton finds the monster hanging over his body. The monster tells of his sufferings and the guilt he feels because of his evil acts. Tied to Frankenstein to the very last, he decides that the only way to find rest is to join his creator in death. He leaps from the ship on to a passing ice raft, intending to immolate himself on the frozen wastes, and disappears into the darkness.

Chapter summaries and commentaries

Volume One, Letters I–IV

Robert Walton is a 28-year-old sea captain who sets out from St Petersburg on a journey to the North Pole. He hopes to find a passage from the Pacific to the Atlantic. He writes letters to his sister, Mrs Saville, in London. This expedition is his ultimate dream, and he is determined that it will succeed. He is worried that he has no friend on the trip to sustain him if it should not work out, or to regulate his passions.

Once embarked on the voyage, things are going well when a strange sighting is made. In the middle of the ocean, on sheets of floating ice, a sleigh is seen. It is driven by what appears to be a human, but of enormous size. The figure disappears, leaving the whole crew in amazement. The next day another sleigh pulls up alongside the ship, on the brink of destruction now, amid the ice. This time its driver is human and asks where the ship is bound. He boards the ship, nearly frozen and completely exhausted. It soon becomes evident that he is tracking the enormous figure whom Walton and his men have seen. Walton learns that the stranger, Victor Frankenstein, is deeply distressed. Walton explains to Frankenstein the purpose of his trip to the north, and it becomes clear what a single-minded and ambitiously driven man Walton is. Frankenstein, seeing in Walton a reflection of his own fatally flawed character, becomes violently agitated and decides to tell Walton his own story to try to change Walton's mind.

Commentary: **Walton is a frame narrator, and these opening letters provide the first part of his narrative. His story is what is known as a frame story — in other words, it is an outer story that contains the main events of the novel. Its intention is to set off and present the main story in the same way as a picture frame is intended to enhance, but not detract from, the picture it surrounds. Shelley uses Walton to introduce many of her key themes and techniques: journeys, pride, uncontrollable passions, madness, breaking accepted/acceptable boundaries, dreams,** friendship, isolation, wild landscapes. She makes clear for us the significant parallels between Frankenstein and Walton.

Volume One, Chapter I

Frankenstein recounts his childhood in a wealthy and respected Swiss family. Born in Naples, Frankenstein enjoys an idyllic early childhood. When he is five years old, his parents adopt an angelic orphan girl, whom they raise as their own. The child, named Elizabeth Lavenza, becomes Frankenstein's sister. He all but worships her; she is his most beautiful and valued possession.

Commentary: **Themes of family, kinship and painful isolation emerge. As the product of a loving, almost ideal family, we expect Frankenstein to reflect these qualities himself. Shelley introduces the idea of caring for children and the helpless; this later becomes important in relation to Frankenstein's attitude to the monster he creates.**

Volume One, Chapter II

After the birth of their second son, Ernest, the Frankensteins move back to Switzerland. Victor has a small but intimate group of friends, including Henry Clerval and Elizabeth. Frankenstein passionately desires to learn the secrets of heaven and earth. For the moment, however, Elizabeth's presence restrains him. He becomes fascinated with the works of Paracelsus, Albertus Magnus and Cornelius Agrippa, a Roman alchemist. He shares their desire to penetrate the secrets of nature. He longs for glory, and wishes to communicate with, or even raise, the dead. He becomes disillusioned with his heroes when he observes a lightning storm, a phenomenon which they are unable to explain.

Commentary: **We see Frankenstein's thirst for forbidden knowledge and his compulsive nature, which comes close to madness. Elizabeth's saintly nature contrasts with Frankenstein's dark desires. The influence of femininity seems to offer potential salvation. Clerval's openness contrasts with Frankenstein's secretive nature, too. Frankenstein's curiosity goes unchecked and undirected by his father. Note Shelley's use of the lightning storm to reflect Frankenstein's situation.**

Context

The corruption of childhood innocence is one of the staple themes of Gothic fiction. The rejection of accepted authority is also typical of Gothic fiction and Romanticism.

Volume One, Chapter III

At 17, Frankenstein goes to Ingolstadt University. Shortly before he leaves home, his mother dies of scarlet fever. She hopes Frankenstein will marry Elizabeth. Clerval wishes to go with Victor to Ingolstadt, but is not allowed. Frankenstein leads a lonely life at the university, but is excited

Task 1

'Liminality' may be defined as an unfixed position between two opposites — the experience of being on a threshold or a boundary. The novel often deals with liminality and trespass, with the boundaries between what is acceptable and what is taboo. Thinking about the idea of trespass in both its legal and its biblical senses, identify occasions when characters cross into forbidden territory — physically, mentally or spiritually.

by his learning. He is almost put off his studies when Krempe ridicules the study he has already undertaken, but is inspired by Waldman, who believes that scientists can perform miracles.

Commentary: **The anticipated companionship of Victor and Elizabeth's marriage contrasts with his isolation at Ingolstadt. Alone, Victor is at the mercy of his own ambitious pursuit of knowledge. Waldman's god-like view of scientists fuels Frankenstein's determination to pursue his studies.**

Volume One, Chapter IV

Frankenstein becomes Waldman's protégé, and is secluded in the laboratory. He does not go home in two years. He becomes consumed by the human frame and the life force. Pillaging graveyards for body parts, he discovers the secret of generating life. He determines to create a new race of beings. The days and nights and seasons pass without Frankenstein noticing. He grows pale and emaciated.

Commentary: **Frankenstein's obsession grows. He becomes increasingly isolated and yearns for god-like powers; he transgresses the boundaries of wise and acceptable research. He becomes increasingly monstrous and appears subhuman in the bloody pursuit of his studies. His declining physical condition reflects his declining moral stature.**

SNAP/Rex Features

Frankenstein finally brings his creature to life, in Kenneth Branagh's 1994 film

Volume One, Chapter V

Frankenstein brings his creation to life. Far from being the beautiful creature he imagined, it is hideous, and Frankenstein at once rushes to his room in horror and disgust. He has difficulty sleeping, and has terrible nightmares about Elizabeth and his mother. He wakes to find the creature staring at him fondly. Frankenstein runs out of his apartment, leaving the creature alone, and unexpectedly meets Clerval. Frankenstein learns of the worries of his family, who have not heard from him for so long. He conceals his work from Clerval. The monster has left, but the next day Frankenstein falls violently ill. Clerval nurses him back to health. A letter awaits Frankenstein from Elizabeth.

Commentary: **The dreaming and waking worlds are blurred in this chapter — it is full of dreams and nightmares, some of which are fantasy and some of which are terribly real. The 'birth' of the monster is a surprisingly subdued event in the text. Frankenstein's sickness of body symbolises his sickness of mind and morality. The creature's innocent and loving approaches to his creator contrast brutally with the rejection and horror Victor feels towards the monster. His cruelty to the monster also contrasts with Clerval's selfless kindness and care.**

Volume One, Chapter VI

Victor resolves to reply at once to Elizabeth. Clerval, seeing Frankenstein's distaste for his laboratory, finds new accommodation and removes all his instruments. Frankenstein decides to return to Geneva, but first he and Clerval undertake a walking tour during which Frankenstein seems to be returning to himself and his old love of nature.

Commentary: **Elizabeth's letter emphasises how complete Frankenstein's isolation in Ingolstadt has been. His sudden abandonment of science is clearly an attempt to deny the events of the last two years. He attempts to forget the existence of the creature to whom he owes so much in the way of care and attention. He refuses to acknowledge his errors and false pride.**

Volume One, Chapter VII

Frankenstein's father writes telling of the murder of his youngest brother, William. He begs Frankenstein to return without delay. A stolen locket provides the ostensible motive. Full of fears, Frankenstein returns to Geneva, arriving in the midst of a terrific thunderstorm. A flash of lightning reveals an enormous figure lurking in some trees. Frankenstein is

---

Taking it **Further**

Watch the events of this chapter in two or three of the film/TV adaptations listed in the *Taking it further* section (pp. 89–92 of this guide). Which do you find the most powerful, and why?

*Pause for **Thought***

Think carefully about Shelley's use of dreams in this chapter. What effects does she achieve through her use of them?

Task 2

Collect a bank of
the vocabulary that
Shelley uses about the
monster. What views of
the creature does this
suggest?

Task 3

Compare and contrast
Shelley's use of the
storm in this chapter
with the storm at the
monster's creation.

Task 4

Imagine you are Justine
Moritz on the eve of
your execution. Write a
journal entry exploring
your beliefs and
feelings. Try to reflect
Shelley's structure, form
and language.

Taking it
Further

How do these four key
ideas of the Romantic
philosopher Rousseau
relate to the major
concerns and events of
Frankenstein?
● the increasing separation
  of Man from Nature
● increasing unhappiness
  and loss of virtue
● society imposes
  restraints on the
  individual
● humans have an innate
  sense of justice and
  virtue

certain that the monster is the murderer. He longs to pursue the creature
and warn his family, but fears that they will think he is mad. He learns
that Justine Moritz, a trusted family servant, is to be tried for the murder.

Commentary: **A lightning storm (a staple device of Gothic horror)
heralds the return of the monster. The storm symbolises the
internal turmoil facing Frankenstein. His language towards the
monster — 'deformity', 'wretch', 'filthy daemon' — sets the tone
for their future relations. Frankenstein disingenuously refuses
to tell his tale of shame, on the grounds that it will be written
off as madness, in order to protect himself and his reputation.**

Volume One, Chapter VIII

Justine's trial commences. Frankenstein considers speaking to save
Justine, but does not. The evidence against her is compelling — she
has the stolen locket. Elizabeth speaks passionately in Justine's defence,
but cannot prevent the inevitable death sentence. To obtain absolution
before she dies, Justine confesses to the crime in prison, even though
she is innocent. Frankenstein selfishly considers his own plight to be
worse than that of Justine.

Commentary: **Justine and William are the first innocent victims of
Frankenstein's ambition. Victor will not or cannot explain the
truth, and is torn by the 'fangs of remorse'. He is isolated in his
terrible suspicions of the truth. Like the monster, his ability to
relate to human society is limited.**

Volume Two, Chapter I

Frankenstein is tormented by guilt. The family retires to Belrive.
Frankenstein contemplates suicide and finds himself out of harmony with
his magnificent surroundings. He nurtures a pathological hatred of his
creation and thinks of nothing but revenge. Elizabeth now sees mankind
as monsters; her views increase Frankenstein's pain. He takes a tour of the
Chamounix valley to try to escape his emotional turmoil.

Commentary: **Frankenstein is isolated emotionally, caught
between his hatred of the monster and his love of his family,
both of which are equally painful to him. Nature plays a
key role: the awesome, God-revealing natural world that
Frankenstein loves is ironically set against his unnatural
rejection of that order in setting himself up as God through
his scientific researches. Elizabeth's view of men as monsters
tellingly questions whether it is Frankenstein or his creature
that is truly monstrous.**

Volume Two, Chapter II

Frankenstein continues his tour of Chamounix. He climbs Montanvert, where he calls on the 'wandering spirits' to help him. At this the monster appears. Frankenstein, in fury, threatens to kill him, but the monster remains rational and asks Frankenstein to help him in his misery, threatening bloody revenge if he fails to do so. The monster is eloquent in presenting his intrinsically good nature and his pitiful isolation in the world. He begs Frankenstein to hear his story.

Commentary: **Frankenstein seeks escape in the rugged wilderness of the mountains. The meeting between creator and creature is loaded with biblical and Miltonic references to the story of Adam, Satan and God.**

Task 5

In the Bible, high places are often related to power and revelation. How do you find these ideas useful in reading *Frankenstein*?

Volume Two, Chapter III

The monster recounts his early development and awareness of the world around him. Tormented by want, the monster resides in the forests near Ingolstadt. Whenever he comes in contact with humans, he suffers maltreatment, in spite of his efforts to befriend them. He finally takes refuge in a hovel by a cottage, where he spends his time observing the inhabitants, the De Laceys.

Commentary: **In this chapter, we enter the heart of the novel — the monster's narrative. Shelley emphasises the early good nature of the monster, which contrasts with the humans he meets and their treatment of him. The monster's innocence and capacity for love are gradually undermined. Isolation is emphasised.**

Volume Two, Chapter IV

The monster admires and loves the De Laceys. He helps them in secret and tries to learn their language. He realises that they are unhappy, but cannot understand why — they possess everything he lacks: love, shelter, companionship. One day, he sees his hideous reflection in a pool, but continues to hope to win them over by the beauty of his soul.

Commentary: **The creature longs to join human society. Comparing himself to the De Laceys, he feels himself to be a monster. Shelley builds pathos as the monster continues to dream of acceptance by humans.**

Volume Two, Chapter V

A beautiful stranger arrives at the cottage. It is Safie, Felix De Lacey's sweetheart. They teach her their language, and unwittingly teach the

monster too. From the history book they use, the creature learns of human cruelty and despairs of gaining the acceptance of the cottagers.

Commentary: **The monster's attractive humanity becomes clear. Safie is another outsider. The monstrosity of human society is emphasised, leading to the monster's despair — both he and Frankenstein are estranged by what they know.**

Volume Two, Chapter VI

The monster learns the family's name and history. Trying to help Safie and her father, imprisoned on account of their race in Paris, the family lost their place in society. Safie was promised in marriage to Felix, but upon gaining freedom, her father betrayed Felix, and Felix's father and sister were imprisoned. They were forced to live in exile in Germany. Safie escaped her father and found her lover.

Commentary: **Shelley places further emphasis on betrayal and the position of the outsider. The story reflects both the goodness and evil of which humans are capable.**

Volume Two, Chapter VII

The monster reads Milton's *Paradise Lost*, Plutarch's *Lives* and Goethe's *The Sorrows of Young Werther*, believing they are fact. He relates his relationship with Victor to Milton's story. Winter comes, and the monster decides to speak to the cottagers. He at first speaks to the blind old man alone. All goes well until the return of Felix and the others, who drive him away.

Commentary: **The books give the monster a way of reading his own situation. His initial rejection by Victor is emphasised by the De Laceys' reaction. Good and evil compete in his mind. His goodness and love have been met with evil and irrational hatred.**

Volume Two, Chapter VIII

The monster curses his creator and declares revenge on mankind. A final effort to engage with the De Laceys is foiled, and he burns their cottage to the ground. He decides to travel to Geneva to exact his revenge. Further encounters, even with innocent children, serve only to confirm what he has already learnt. On arriving near Geneva, he meets a child (Frankenstein's brother), kills him and steals his locket, which he hides on Justine Moritz. The monster demands that Frankenstein create a companion for him, so he will no longer be alone.

Context

Isolation and imprisonment are common features of Gothic fiction. Ann Radcliffe's heroines are frequently trapped in castles, caverns or dark forests. There are noteworthy scenes of imprisonment in *Dracula* (e.g. when Jonathan Harker visits the Count's castle) and in *The Monk* (by Matthew Lewis). Psychological imprisonment is also important — the mentally entrapped Renfield, in *Dracula*, is incarcerated in an asylum, and the protagonist of James Hogg's novel *The Private Memoirs and Confessions of a Justified Sinner* is captured within the labyrinth of his own mind.

Commentary: **The burning of the cottage is an externalisation of the fire of revenge now burning in the monster's heart. The violence of the landscapes he passes through and of the elements further reflect the monster's state of mind.**

Volume Two, Chapter IX

Frankenstein returns as narrator. Initially he refuses the monster's demand, fearing the consequences, but the monster persuades Frankenstein that he has a duty to make him a companion. Frankenstein is full of doubts, but feels compassion and decides to comply. The monster vows to watch his progress. Frankenstein returns to Geneva.

Commentary: **The monster is much more reasonable and controlled than Frankenstein. The monster is aware that he is more powerful than his creator and is therefore, in a sense, the master. In conceding to the creature's demands, Frankenstein implicitly accepts responsibility for his actions.**

Volume Three, Chapter I

Frankenstein cannot steel himself to begin his dreadful task. Before going to England to undertake the necessary study and work, he agrees to marry Elizabeth on his return. As he travels with Clerval, he is continually aware of the monster's haunting presence. Frankenstein is painfully aware of the differences between himself and Clerval.

Commentary: **Marriage is again important. Frankenstein's forthcoming union parallels the monster's anticipated union with a new companion; the two are linked in our minds. Frankenstein is as bound to the monster and his promise as a slave.**

*Pause for **Thought***

Consider the various marriages and unions in the novel. What effects does Shelley achieve by comparing and contrasting them?

Volume Three, Chapter II

After a protracted tour, Frankenstein leaves Clerval and takes a cottage on a remote, barren island to complete his second creation.

Commentary: **Frankenstein's ability to take pleasure is blasted. He is increasingly aware of his separation from the rest of mankind.**

Volume Three, Chapter III

Frankenstein contemplates the possible outcomes of complying with the monster's wishes. He sees the grinning face of the monster watching him, and then and there destroys the body he is creating. The creature disappears, but returns several hours later to reproach Frankenstein.

Top ten **quotation** ❯

Taking it ➤
Further

Find out what a doppelgänger is. Can you think of any examples from books that you have read or films that you have seen? How does this relate to Frankenstein and the monster?

He expresses the central paradox of their relationship: 'You are my creator, but I am your master.' The monster leaves, vowing to be with Frankenstein on his wedding night. Frankenstein disposes of the destroyed body at sea. He drifts on the current, landing on the Irish coast. In the meantime, a dead man has been found on the shore, and Frankenstein is arrested on suspicion of murder.

Commentary: **Frankenstein faces a terrible dilemma — the humanitarian responsibility of meeting his creature's needs and the selfish desire to destroy. He mistakenly attributes the monster's threats to himself alone. The balance between power and weakness, control and obedience in the complex relationship between creator and creature is multiplied. In many ways, Frankenstein and the monster are inseparable.**

Volume Three, Chapter IV

Frankenstein is taken before the magistrate and shown the body of Clerval, his supposed victim. For two months, Frankenstein is delirious. During his illness, Frankenstein's father travels to Ireland. Frankenstein insists on returning to Geneva at once to protect the rest of his family.

Commentary: **Note the parallels between Frankenstein's 'murder' of the monster's companion and the murder of Clerval. Note, too, how Shelley prepares the way for Elizabeth's murder.**

Volume Three, Chapter V

Frankenstein tells his father that he is the cause of the family's tragedy, but his father attributes this confession to his son's delirium. Frankenstein decides not to delay his marriage to Elizabeth in spite of the monster's warnings. He believes that he can avert the monster's threats and live happily with Elizabeth.

Commentary: **Frankenstein's self-delusion and solipsism are key here. He persists in believing that the monster's threat is to him. Note Shelley's juxtaposition of happiness and a brooding sense of foreboding. Note, too, Frankenstein's comparison to Adam and Eve, alerting us to the inevitable presence of Satan (the monster).**

solipsism the theory that the self is the only thing that can be known and verified

Volume Three, Chapter VI

Frankenstein and Elizabeth arrive in Como. Frankenstein, certain that either he or the creature will die that night, sends Elizabeth to bed to try to protect her. Too late he hears her death screams. He embraces Elizabeth's corpse, then sees the monster at the window, gloating over his grief. A search for the monster fails. Frankenstein's father dies shortly after hearing the news. Frankenstein admits all to a half-believing magistrate, but is left to pursue his revenge alone.

Commentary: **Note the use of the natural world to reflect events. Frankenstein is blinded by his solipsism to the true intentions of the monster. Frankenstein and his monster are drawn closer together than ever — both are isolated, consumed with revenge.**

Volume Three, Chapter VII

Frankenstein vows eternal revenge. He visits the graves of his family and is watched and taunted by the monster. For months he pursues his creation, until at last he sights it on the northern ocean. When he is on the point of catching the monster, the ice breaks and he is adrift on an ice floe, where he is rescued by Walton. He begs Walton to kill the monster if he appears.

Commentary: **Revenge invigorates and intoxicates Frankenstein. Note how he calls upon the 'wandering ministers of vengeance' and the spirits of the dead to aid him. He buries guilt in anger.**

Walton, *in continuation*

Walton questions Frankenstein on how he created life. Frankenstein grows agitated and begs Walton to learn from his tale. Walton becomes increasingly attached to Frankenstein. Meanwhile, the ship is every day in greater danger from the encroaching ice. Walton is unwilling to accept the crew's desire to return if the ice breaks. Frankenstein is torn between the desire to save Walton from his fate and the urge to enlist his assistance in pursuing revenge, and offers a range of contradictory pleas and advice. Frankenstein dies, stating that his conduct has been blameless. That night, the monster steals on to the ship and laments over the corpse of Frankenstein, aware, in Frankenstein's death, of the pain his acts of revenge have caused. Walton meets the monster and is unable to express the ambiguity of his emotions. The monster jumps from the ship, intending to burn himself alive at the North Pole.

Commentary: **Frankenstein appears to have learnt nothing from his sufferings and dies desiring revenge and still extolling the possibilities of scientific research. It is uncertain whether Walton will learn his lesson or not. The monster alone shows firm evidence of moral betterment. The novel ends with the suggestive combination of fire and ice.**

Task **6**

Think of occasions in the novel when characters either look out of places they do not wish to be or look in on places where they do wish to be. Take two or three of these situations and compare the effects Shelley achieves through them.

---

*Pause for **Thought***

How free are the characters within this novel to act independently, and how far are they imprisoned and at the mercy of forces beyond their control?

Task **7**

Imagine you are writing a new screen adaptation of *Frankenstein*. Write the final scene of your adaptation. You may choose to focus on Frankenstein and Walton, or the monster, or both.

Themes

The elements

In a novel which deals with power and raw, elemental emotion, it is not surprising that Shelley makes extensive use of the elements. The power of the natural world is an apt representation of the characters' shifting emotions. These are often externalised using the elements, as when Frankenstein observes after Elizabeth's murder: 'The sun might shine, or the clouds might lower: but nothing could appear to me as it had done the day before' (p. 201).

The four humours are significant here. Blood, phlegm, choler (anger) and melancholy (or black choler) are linked to the elements of earth, air, fire and water. The ideal temperament was believed to be one which contained all four humours in balance, while the preponderance of any one of them led to an imbalance and a consequent failing in character. Shelley's use of the elements is therefore highly significant, especially her deployment of pathetic fallacy (use of the weather or the landscape to reflect events, moods, etc.) to create atmosphere. The most striking use of the elements occurs at moments in the novel where rationality and balance are least in evidence.

The elements are a central part of the nature that Frankenstein loves so deeply. At times, however, they are also part of his punishment. The physical punishment of cold and exposure on the sea of ice, for example, and the hardship of the elements on the Scottish isle, are like divine retribution for his presumption and foolhardiness. Thunder and lightning storms are particularly important in this respect. The 'most violent and terrible thunder-storm' (p. 42) that Frankenstein experiences on returning to Switzerland begins a thread of elemental imagery which runs to the heart of the novel. The power of the electrical storm makes possible Frankenstein's experiments with galvanism and the creation of the monster; the awesome, destructive power of the storm represents the destructive power of Frankenstein's own desires.

Nature

Shelley had very close connections with the Romantic school, which was profoundly engaged with the natural world. Her husband, Percy Bysshe Shelley, was one of the great Romantic poets, as was his close friend

Lord Byron. Wordsworth was also a major figure, and Samuel Taylor Coleridge's *The Rime of the Ancient Mariner* had a particularly profound influence on the novel (see pp. 43–45 of this guide).

For the Romantics, the natural world, with its abundance, wildness and creative excess, was an apt symbol of everything that they admired and wished to promote. They rejected what they saw as the restrictions of balance, order, proportion and objectivity, and profoundly mistrusted the advances of empirical science. The influence of these ideas on Shelley is significant. Frankenstein, the empirical scientist, seeks to apply rigid, scientific rules to the act of creativity, producing an object not beautiful, but hideous.

The range of extreme and dangerous locations that Shelley employs reflects the nature of her tale, and the perilous moral dilemmas it deals with. These locations and landscapes also resonate with the key themes of isolation, death and destruction. They symbolise the inner turmoil and upheaval of the monster, Frankenstein and other characters. They also provide a suitable backdrop to the extraordinary and lurid events she relates. Frankenstein recognises as much when he observes: 'Were we among the tamer scenes of nature, I might fear to encounter your unbelief, perhaps your ridicule; but many things will appear possible in these wild and mysterious regions, which would provoke the laughter of those unacquainted with the ever-varied powers of nature' (p. 31).

Ambiguous nature — beautifully creative, but also powerfully destructive — is key to understanding Frankenstein. He employs the image of a mountain stream to introduce the tale of his downfall, and it is his inability to maintain a sensible relationship with the natural world that leads to his inevitable destruction. His 'unnatural' passions blight for ever his relations with nature. At times he is 'elevated…from all littleness of feeling' (p. 99) and 'diverted' (p. 99) by the beauties of the world around him, at others he is brought face to face with 'the awful and majestic in nature' (p. 100), and at others he is physically tormented by it.

Taking it **Further**

Watch two or three different film adaptations of the novel. How do the directors use the elements to create effect and to reflect events?

Good and evil

The tale is an exploration of good and evil. It dissects the complex interaction of good and evil in the human soul. The concept of 'original sin', central to the biblical narrative and *Paradise Lost*, is at the very heart of *Frankenstein*. The novel explores how good can be turned into evil; the monster, initially a benevolent and loving creature, is transformed by human maltreatment into the ravening and vengeful beast of popular imagination. It also considers the potential of human science and human nature for both good and evil. In this sense, the novel is a kind of morality tale.

Good and evil and their physical manifestations in *Frankenstein* suggest the existence of spiritual powers greater than man which influence the world. Shelley's literary sources also underline the supra-human powers at work in the world — the angelic realms of *Paradise Lost*, the supernatural incursions of *The Rime of the Ancient Mariner* and the Greek deities of the Prometheus myth all emphasise this, and clarify the dangers inherent in Victor's forbidden pursuits.

Death and destruction

Death, destruction, putrefaction and disease are closely linked in the novel. From early on we know that Frankenstein cannot survive for long after his rescue from the drifting ice; he is mortally ill. Death constantly hangs over events; one by one Frankenstein's family die at the hands of the monster. It is ironic, however, that these deaths spring from Frankenstein's driving desire to create life.

Symbolism is again important here. In thoughtlessly neglecting his creation, Frankenstein unleashes a dreadful threat on the world, a monster bent on avenging himself on his creator and humanity. This emphasises the fragility of human existence. Physical death and destruction reflect the death of Frankenstein's moral responsibility and the destruction of his hopes and dreams, and the consequential breakdown of the monster's innocence. It is therefore entirely fitting that the novel should end with the deaths of both creator and creature.

The contrast between the mortal and the immortal is useful here. *Paradise Lost* and the Prometheus myth both examine this closely. Frankenstein dreams of immortality (he wishes to be remembered for ever for his scientific achievements), but is made crushingly aware of his mortality. He usurps immortal God and suffers the consequences. Similarly, Prometheus transgresses the natural relationship between the gods and humanity and is punished.

Even life becomes a kind of death for both monster and Frankenstein; the monster says: '[I am] thy creature, to whom thou art bound by ties only dissoluble by the annihilation of one of us' (p. 102).

Pause for *Thought*

The connections between life and death in *Frankenstein* are complex. What does Shelley's view of this connection seem to be, and how does she explore this in the novel?

The supernatural

The supernatural in *Frankenstein* is unusual. While the novel fits within the Gothic genre, which frequently deals with the supernatural, and refers to the supernatural on many occasions, it does not actually deal with ghosts and spirits but with an all too hard reality. The monster is superhuman — bigger, stronger and in every way larger than his human counterparts — but not supernatural. The horrible power of Shelley's tale lies in the very fact that the monster is flesh and blood.

Frankenstein does not employ the conventional supernatural of novels such as *The Castle of Otranto*, *The Monk* and *Melmoth the Wanderer*, all classic Gothic tales. Nor does it employ the 'explained supernatural' technique favoured by Ann Radcliffe, where occurrences which appear to be supernatural are given a rational explanation at last. Shelley makes clear from the outset that this is no such tale — unless we accept the reality of the monster, the novel loses its power to frighten and warn.

Sir Walter Scott writes of using the supernatural:

> **...the supernatural in fictitious composition requires to be managed with considerable delicacy...The marvellous, more than any other attribute of fictitious narrative, loses its effect by being brought much into view. The imagination of the reader is to be excited if possible, without being gratified. If once, like Macbeth, we 'sup full with horrors', our taste for the banquet is ended, and the thrill of terror with which we hear or read of a night-shriek, becomes lost.**

It is important to note how restrained Shelley is in presenting the monster. With the exception of Frankenstein's brief description, the text is surprisingly lacking in grotesque physical description and details. Scott, Radcliffe and Edmund Burke all recognise how fear emerges from the imperfectly perceived. In refusing to define the monster fully, Shelley allows her reader to paint in the rest of the picture and to create the thing that is for them the most horrible.

Note how Shelley's characters react to events. Although the monster is a creature of flesh and blood with genuine human emotions, they often react as if he were a ghost. As he stalks Frankenstein across Europe, he shares many ghost-like qualities, and can be compared to other great Gothic wanderers, such as Melmoth, the Wandering Jew and Dracula.

Other typical supernatural elements are imported into the text through Shelley's use of *The Rime of the Ancient Mariner*. This poem uses the supernatural extensively and provides supernatural colour to the events of *Frankenstein*. *Paradise Lost*, with its world of angels and demons, likewise imports a dimension of the supernatural.

Pause for **Thought**

Shelley explores the dangers (monsters) facing her own society. What are the monsters that threaten contemporary society?

Pause for **Thought**

Think of recent examples of the supernatural in film, in fiction, on television and on the stage. How is the supernatural represented? What influence does the supernatural continue to have in the twenty-first-century world? How do you think this differs from Shelley's time?

Task 8

How does each of the following examples illustrate Shelley's use of dreams?

1 I try in vain…beauty and delight. (p. 15)

2 [Clerval's] hope and his dream… benefactors of our species. (p. 39)

3 No one can conceive…body to corruption. (p. 55)

4 I slept, indeed…folds of flannel. (p. 59)

5 …I was overcome… rooted to the spot. (p. 172)

6 The whole series… force of reality. (p. 182)

7 O blessed sleep!… fulfil my pilgrimage. (pp. 207–08)

Dreams

Dreams are important in two ways: first, as hopes and aspirations; secondly, as sleeping visions. For Victor, these impinge upon each other — in trying to live out his aspirations as a scientist, he creates a living nightmare.

Characters' dreams

Frankenstein

Frankenstein's dreams vary widely: he dreams of learning the secret of creation; he imagines the wonderful, paternal relationship he will have with the new race of beings he wishes to create; he desires fame; he dreams of benefiting humanity; he dreams of marrying Elizabeth Lavenza; later, he dreams ardently of destroying the monster; he wishes longingly for freedom from the terrible punishment he has brought upon himself, and even contemplates the ultimate liberation of death and suicide; he creates a fantasy around the nuclear family which the monster is gradually stealing from him; he suffers from a disturbing nightmare about Elizabeth and his mother. The destruction of Frankenstein's scientific dreams is mirrored in the destruction of his domestic dreams.

Walton

Walton imagines finding an alternative northern shipping route; partly he desires to aid mankind, but he also dreams of personal fame; his letters make clear his dream of finding lasting and meaningful companionship.

The monster

The monster dreams unceasingly of finding companionship, first with humans, then with a companion whom Frankenstein will create for him; he desires acceptance and love, primarily from his creator, but also from society at large; he dreams of finding the basic necessities, such as food and shelter; his dreams are perpetually shattered, perhaps most crushingly when the De Laceys reject him; becoming embittered, he dreams of exacting revenge upon Frankenstein.

Elizabeth

Elizabeth dreams of Frankenstein's return; her view of him is some kind of fantasy, as in spite of his numerous failings she seems unaware of his true nature.

Felix De Lacey

Felix wishes to be reunited with Safie; he also dreams of attaining happiness for his family.

Sanity and insanity

On many occasions in the novel we question the sanity of what we observe, and the characters often do so themselves. Frankenstein's and Walton's frantic pursuit of their dreams creates an atmosphere of unpredictability and fear. At the outset Frankenstein alerts us to the unbelievable (insane?) nature of his story. The persistent presence of madness also serves to emphasise the danger inherent in Frankenstein's and Walton's enterprises. The novel maintains its threatening atmosphere by treading the fine line between insanity (fantasy) and sanity (reality).

Revenge

Frankenstein and the monster are locked in an endless cycle of vengeance. Frankenstein's refusal to recognise and care for his creature makes this inevitable. The monster wishes to avenge the lack of care and love that he rightly believes are his due; a responsible creator must care for his creature. Frankenstein's failure to do this leads to the monster's isolation and loneliness. As Satan does in the biblical narrative of Genesis and in *Paradise Lost*, the monster seeks his revenge not directly by attacking the creator, but indirectly through attacking those most dear to him. Frankenstein is the particular object of his revenge, but as all humans reject him, he seeks vengeance on all humanity (e.g. when he frames Justine Moritz for William's murder). In his turn, Frankenstein wishes for vengeance, seeking to destroy his creation.

Exploration

Frankenstein is full of explorers and exploration. Victor Frankenstein's scientific research is a type of exploration; Walton is exploring the Arctic Circle; Frankenstein's work is based on the explorations of Galvani; Paracelsus, Albertus Magnus, Krempe, Waldman and the other scientists at Ingolstadt are also explorers. Beyond this, Shelley explores unknown tracts of human experience and the dark recesses of the mind and soul. Nearly a century before the psychoanalysts Sigmund Freud and Carl Jung, Shelley explores the divided self and the shadowy world of dreams, where sanity and insanity merge. The novel is also exploratory in that it breaks new ground, taking Gothic into new psychological depths and paving the way for science fiction.

Task 9

The mad scientist is an archetypal character. Is this a fair way of viewing Frankenstein? Collect and consider Shelley's language and explore how this affects our views of him.

Imprisonment and confinement

Frankenstein finds himself increasingly imprisoned within dreams and fantasies that resolve into nightmarish reality. He finds himself trapped in a relationship with the monster and ethically bound by a set of responsibilities that he disastrously proceeds to ignore. As the relationship with the monster deteriorates, both creator and creature find themselves prisoners within an unbreakable and deadly cycle of hatred and revenge. Frankenstein is a prisoner of his own imagination and is trapped within the workings of his own mind. He is literally imprisoned in Ireland as the suspected murderer of Clerval.

The monster, rejected by Frankenstein and repeatedly a victim of prejudice, is trapped in isolation, revenge and hatred. His noble, affectionate personality cannot escape the ugliness of his body. The hovel next to the De Laceys' cottage is a pathetic symbol of his confinement. The monster's rejection is universal, and as such the whole world is a prison to him.

Elizabeth is imprisoned in her relationship with Frankenstein, which is doomed to fruitlessness and death. Blinded by his own egotism (or wilful ignorance of the intentions of the monster), Frankenstein locks Elizabeth in their room on their wedding night in an attempt to protect her. Justine Moritz is gaoled for William's murder. Safie and her father are incarcerated as aliens in Paris, the victims of racial discrimination. M. De Lacey is trapped in a world of darkness by his blindness, although ironically this temporarily leaves him free to appreciate the monster's amiable nature. Beyond this, all humanity is imprisoned in ignorance and prejudice, unable to see beyond the monster's unpromising exterior to the genuinely loving and good nature this conceals.

> Frankenstein is a prisoner of his own imagination

Human and inhuman

Humans are frequently guilty of the greatest ingratitude and inhumanity, both towards the monster and towards other human beings, whilst the monster frequently demonstrates kindness, humility and the potential for love. Shelley's treatment of this issue causes us to question how far humans are humane and how far they are, in fact, monstrous.

> Shelley...causes us to question how far humans are humane and how far they are, in fact, monstrous

Loneliness and isolation

All the major characters suffer from this. Frankenstein isolates himself first from his family and then from his fellow researchers in the university, leading to his disastrous creation of the monster. On his voyage north, Walton laments his isolation and lack of companionship. The monster cannot enter society because of his horrific appearance. Clerval, left alone by Frankenstein on their journey to Scotland, is murdered. Elizabeth is left alone by Frankenstein for extended periods of time, and is left fatally isolated on their wedding night. Justine Moritz, lonely and gaoled for a crime she did not commit, is threatened with permanent separation from God by a bullying priest. Safie is isolated in Paris, abandoned by her father, then forced to travel alone. The De Laceys become social outcasts when Safie's father betrays them. Notice also Shelley's predilection for isolated and lonely locations, which reflect the pervasive loneliness and isolation of her characters.

Ambition and determination

Sometimes this is laudable, sometimes less so. Frankenstein and Walton are ambitiously determined in pursuing their dreams; Frankenstein is also doggedly determined in chasing down the monster. The monster shows great determination in learning language, in surviving against the odds and in attempting to persuade Frankenstein to fulfil his responsibilities; when this fails, he is equally determined in revenge. In the face of injustice, Justine Moritz remains determined and proud, as does Elizabeth. Clerval does not allow his desire to study to be deflected by his father's initial refusal, and he is unstintingly loyal to Victor. The De Laceys and Safie demonstrate great strength of character in the face of considerable hardships.

Journeys

Frankenstein, his father, Walton, Elizabeth, Clerval, the monster, Safie and the De Laceys all undertake journeys, sometimes repeated and of considerable length. In the later stages of the tale, Frankenstein and the monster are engaged in a perpetual journey. These journeys have both a literal and a symbolic importance. The physical journeys undertaken, often into rugged, inhospitable and foreign terrain, reflect the characters' psychological journeys.

The physical journeys undertaken... reflect the characters' psychological journeys

Science

Shelley never passes explicit moral judgement on scientific research, but implicitly her tale is a powerful moral warning of the potential dangers of unrestrained and thoughtless experimentation. Frankenstein never

repents of his scientific research, only the consequences of it; even at the last he will not warn Walton unequivocally of the dangers he faces, looking to the possibility that another may succeed where he has failed. He sees science as an afflicting disease, evidence of which he also sees in the character of Walton. Walton's return to Archangel at the end of the novel is highly ambivalent — the reader is given no indication of the eventual fate of Walton and his crew, and whether he does see sense and alter his course (literally and metaphorically) in the light of Frankenstein's tale.

In the monster, we have a grotesque symbol of the outcomes of irresponsible scientific experimentation. He stalks the pages of the novel like some gruesome laboratory animal, a composite and bastard creation made up of reconstructed cadavers.

Walton and Frankenstein illustrate the dangers of working without the sensible checks and balances a companion would provide.

While she provides a salutary warning, Shelley does not appear to be entirely opposed to the pursuit of science.

Noble science

There are clear signs in the novel that the pursuit of science can be both noble and ennobling. The ability to explore and to analyse the world in which we live symbolises the power of the human intellect, and at its best it elevates the individual and improves the mass of humanity. Both Frankenstein and Walton begin their explorations in the hope of benefiting the world through their work. To the end, indeed, they maintain some vestige of the hope of using their discoveries to improve the lot of mankind. Frankenstein initially aspires to finding a way of preserving life, while Walton wishes to find a quicker and safer trading route than those currently used by sailors.

Dangerous science

While Shelley is never overtly critical of the practice of science, she is keenly alert to its many potential pitfalls and dangers. Science seeks to extend the bounds of human knowledge, and this extension of the frontiers of conventional understanding is risky; it leads to moral choices, which may or may not be made sensibly. Walton and Frankenstein both operate at the edges of human experience, and require self-knowledge, assurance and self-control. Both men, however, struggle to curtail their passion. They are swayed by arrogant desire, and anticipation and excitement act on them like a drug. Hearing of Walton's dreams of finding a polar passage, Frankenstein observes: 'Unhappy man! Do you

share my madness? Have you drunk also of the intoxicating draught?'
(p. 29). It is an intoxication that can lead to reckless experimentation,
as Walton identifies: 'What can stop the determined heart and resolved
will of man?' (p. 24). Neither man has the ability to impose balance
— the image of intoxication is very appropriate here. Their unchecked
determination and resolution lead to dangerously unbalanced emotions.

The monster symbolises the destructive potential of irresponsible
science. Rejected immediately after his creation, he is released on the
world without a thought to his welfare and his future development. He is
a bastard creation, incapable of integrating into society by himself, and
as such he develops into the scourge of his creator. As a result,
Frankenstein's view of the natural world is for ever jaundiced; once a
great lover of nature, after the creation of the monster he is incapable of
maintaining an 'innocent' relationship with the world and God. The
monster symbolises his uncontrollable thirst for knowledge, externalising
his monstrous desires and their hideous potential.

The frontispiece to the
1831 edition of the novel
shows Frankenstein
abandoning his creation
in horror

Scientists in the novel

Frankenstein

From his teenage years, Frankenstein is fascinated with the natural world and wishes to understand the processes behind the beauty he sees. His early studies are a confused conglomeration of ideas from the natural sciences and the bizarre alchemical writings of Albertus Magnus and Paracelsus. Although his father rejects them, Frankenstein continues to immerse himself in these authors and takes a place at Ingolstadt, where Waldman's lecture on the power of modern scientists fascinates him. He is respected by his fellows in the university but, unable to check his desires, strays into dangerous areas of research, culminating in the creation of the monster. He offers his cautionary, but not unambiguous, tale to Walton.

Captain Robert Walton

Like Frankenstein, Walton is a determined explorer. He is fired by enthusiasm and apparently reckless of the consequences. He is drawn to Frankenstein, recognising in him a man of very similar temperament. His response to Frankenstein's cautionary tale is ambiguous; he is moved by it and laments Victor's tragic fate, but still retains the desire to press on with his journey at the end of the novel. It is only under duress that he grudgingly consents to return to Archangel.

Krempe

Krempe is 'deeply imbued in the secrets of his science'. Frankenstein finds him conceited and condescending as he mocks Paracelsus's and Albertus Magnus's achievements. This serves only to strengthen Frankenstein's determination. Krempe does not inspire Frankenstein, but works unwittingly alongside Waldman in setting him on his path to destruction.

Waldman

Waldman is a passionate enthusiast who awakens Frankenstein to the possibilities of modern chemistry. His evaluation of the state of modern science, where the scientists 'ascend into the heavens' and develop 'new and almost unlimited powers', fires Frankenstein's desire to be a great scientist.

Paracelsus and Albertus Magnus

Paracelsus and Albertus Magnus are Frankenstein's first encounter with the world of science. He is fascinated by their writings, even though his father rejects them as 'sad trash' (p. 40) and Krempe refers to their work as 'a desert land', 'exploded systems', 'a thousand years old and as musty as they are ancient' (p. 47). They write of the raising of spirits and other supernatural phenomena, possibilities which become a terrible reality embodied in the monster.

Science and taboo

Shelley demonstrates that the human race is on the brink of the unknown, and questions the wisdom of pressing heedlessly into it for fear of the 'monsters' that may emerge. Shelley's use of Milton and the stories of Adam and Eve and Prometheus suggests the forbidden nature of the scientific discoveries that Frankenstein pursues. Like Adam and Eve, he finds himself tempted to reach for the forbidden. He wants to push on to enter the secret citadels of science.

Frankenstein's interest in alchemy illustrates his aspiration and determination to push at the barriers in his pursuit of the secret of life. Alchemists searched for the Philosopher's Stone and the Elixir of Life, both supposedly sources of eternal life, as well as seeking to turn base metal into gold. All of these things clearly attract Frankenstein, who seeks the source of life and hopes through his researches to ensure the perpetuity of his reputation and fame. He is not afraid of the consequences of his actions, seeing only the potential glory that may accrue to him. Alchemy was, of course, by Shelley's time a discredited system of scientific thought. This in itself is suggestive, demonstrating to the reader the likely outcomes of Frankenstein's pursuits.

At the end of his life, Frankenstein recognises something of the error of his ways and the impact the pursuit of the forbidden has had upon him. He observes to Walton:

> **A human being in perfection ought always to preserve a calm and peaceful mind, and never to allow passion or a transitory desire to disturb his tranquillity. I do not think that the pursuit of knowledge is an exception to this rule. If the study to which you apply yourself has a tendency to weaken your affections, and to destroy your taste for those simple pleasures in which no alloy can possibly mix, then that study is certainly unlawful, that is to say, not befitting the human mind. (p. 56)**

In a similar vein, he refers to the monster as 'the result of my curiosity and lawless devices' (p. 83). He recognises that he has transgressed and that not only he but others suffer as a result.

Shelley...questions the wisdom of pressing heedlessly into the unknown for fear of the 'monsters' that may emerge

He is not afraid of the consequences of his actions, seeing only the potential glory that may accrue to him

Characters

Character outlines

Victor Frankenstein

Frankenstein is a complex and fascinating character, and we have some difficulty in deciding whether he is a hero or a villain. While his ends are evil, he is in many ways more misguided and deluded than actually evil. He is far from being the conventional villain of the Gothic world, displaying all too clearly the weaknesses and frailties of his nature. He is, however, indirectly responsible for causing the doom of his entire family and the monster he has created. Throughout the novel we gain a strange sense of the relationship between Frankenstein and the typical Gothic hero-villain, a role which he curiously subverts.

There is a distinct sense in which Frankenstein also relates to the figure of the Gothic heroine. Gothic novels often focus on the perspective of the heroine, exploring the psychological impact of repeated terror, horror and stress. Typically, the impact of events is manifested in bodily and mental breakdown. As Frankenstein suffers his just deserts at the hands of the monster, his mental and physical decay are evident.

Immediately after the successful creation of the monster, for example, he breaks down entirely, only surviving thanks to the good graces of his friend Clerval. As a study in the psychological impact of the terrible and the horrible, this confusion of the roles of hero/villain/heroine in Frankenstein is compelling.

The monster

Like Frankenstein, the monster is a complex and fascinating character. There are strong arguments for seeing him as an extension of his creator (see also pp. 30 and 45 of this guide). As with Frankenstein, the monster's role is strikingly ambiguous: to what extent is he the traditional villain and to what extent is he the victim of the piece? There is no doubt that as the novel progresses he grows increasingly villainous and malign, manipulating the doom of others with gloating satisfaction in his insatiable pursuit of revenge. The motivation for his actions, however, mitigates our view. In many ways he is the helpless and friendless victim,

Taking it
Further

Watch Kenneth Branagh's film adaptation of the novel, made in 1994, which is called *Mary Shelley's Frankenstein*. How does his representation of the character of Victor Frankenstein and of the novel in general relate to your understanding of the original text?

Pause for **Thought**

As the novel progresses, how does Shelley demonstrate the changes that come over Frankenstein? What is the impact of these changes on those around him?

a role traditionally given within the framework of Gothic to a young woman or child.

Elizabeth Lavenza

Elizabeth is clearly the heroine. Her role, however, like so many of the characters in the novel, bears certain striking discrepancies from the conventions of Gothic. Unlike her counterparts in the works of Ann Radcliffe and Matthew Lewis, Elizabeth's role is comparatively small. Like them she inevitably suffers at the hands of Frankenstein and the monster, but the main focus of the text is not her ordeals, but rather those faced by Frankenstein, her supposed protector and hero, within whose suffering her own is subsumed. She is an undeniably strong woman — far stronger, we suspect, than Frankenstein himself. She faces the repeated trials imposed upon her by Frankenstein with an unswerving loyalty and heroic resolve.

The horrific image of her white-clad body draped across the marital bed after her murder on the wedding night is pure Gothic sensation, however, and a turning point in our understanding of her role, as we realise that she has in fact been the typical Gothic heroine of her own tale which runs parallel to Frankenstein's, in which she is the victim of neglect and systematic cruelty.

Henry Clerval

Clerval embodies many of the heroic qualities that Victor Frankenstein lacks. Like the monster and Walton, he must be seen alongside the central figure of Frankenstein. He draws on some of the characteristics of the good male of Gothic fiction, the man (usually young and good-looking) who attempts to save the heroine from the trials to which she is subjected.

Captain Walton

Walton is something of the dashing, Romantic hero. He is clearly a representation of what Frankenstein used to be before his terrible confrontation with the monster. He fulfils a typical role within the realms of Gothic fiction, appearing as a younger, 'innocent' version of the hero.

Minor characters

Frankenstein Senior: Loving and caring; emotional; fails to control Frankenstein's budding scientific ambition; his parenting contrasts with Frankenstein's 'parenting' of the monster.

Taking it Further

Read selections from classic Gothic novels such as *The Monk*, *The Castle of Otranto*, *The Mysteries of Udolpho*, *Dracula* and *The Strange Case of Dr Jekyll and Mr Hyde*. What similarities and differences do you identify between them?

Frankenstein's mother: Loving; caring; a powerful influence, even after death, on her family and Frankenstein in particular.

Justine Moritz: Upright; devoted; her unjust accusation of murder parallels Frankenstein's unjust accusation of having murdered Clerval.

The De Laceys: Outsiders; kind and caring; ultimate rejection of monster.

Safie: Outsider; exotic stranger; determined; devoted.

William: Innocent victim; shows how even children reject the monster.

Krempe: Disliked by Frankenstein; almost unwittingly 'saves' Frankenstein.

Waldman: Passionate scientist; wins Frankenstein for science.

Taking it **Further**

For classic examples of the doppelgänger, read Robert Louis Stevenson's *The Strange Case of Dr Jekyll and Mr Hyde* or Fyodor Dostoevsky's *The Double*.

Pairings

Typically in Gothic fiction, an ostensibly 'good' character is shadowed by a more sinister, even ghostly, double, or doppelgänger, which is usually taken to represent the darker potential of their nature. Shelley makes extensive use of pairs of characters. These pairings are not necessarily fixed; indeed, they shift frequently as the novel progresses, creating a range of different effects and pointing out both similarities and differences between characters.

Frankenstein and the monster

Both Frankenstein and the monster begin life with the potential for good, but find their lives turned to evil. Shelley develops a complex series of parallels between the creator and his creature. As Frankenstein dumps the body of his aborted companion for the monster in the sea, so the monster dumps the body of Clerval in the sea. Both Frankenstein and the monster find themselves increasingly isolated from the companionship of mankind. Both rebel against their creators. Both share the physical hardship and torment of their ceaseless pursuit across Europe, a vengeful pursuit which consumes both the body and the spirit. The mutually destructive passion that fires both man and monster reaches its heights of vindictive fury in the destruction of each other's 'brides'. Both are guilty of committing crimes against humanity, which they have to pay for in their increasing isolation and consuming guilt. Through these extended parallels, the two characters are tied to each other inseparably. The distinctions between Frankenstein and the monster become increasingly blurred — to the extent that they are at times indistinguishable.

Frankenstein and Walton

Both men are dreamers, blinded by their fantasies to the truth and the impact of what they are seeking to achieve. Shelley uses the apparently more rational figure of Walton as a foil to Frankenstein, who may otherwise appear as an insane and extreme scientific renegade. While he shares Frankenstein's obsessive personality and desire to reach new heights (or depths) of scientific research, Walton is as yet comparatively innocent and unaware of the potential consequences of his actions. This pairing prepares us for the transformation of Frankenstein from the scientist with a dream to the fear-crazed madman whom Walton encounters on the ice.

An almost spiritual closeness exists between Walton and Frankenstein. Walton senses in Frankenstein a kindred spirit; however, we must note that the friendship Walton describes cannot be forged with Frankenstein in his current state — it is the former Frankenstein who might have proved a fit companion for him. This serves to illustrate the imminent danger facing Walton should he continue along the path he is currently treading. Both Walton and Frankenstein have difficulties with self-control, single-mindedly pursuing their dreams even in the face of warnings to the contrary. As such, Frankenstein's tale is a cautionary lesson for Walton.

The closeness between the two men is driven home at the end of the novel, when Frankenstein seeks to use Walton as an extension of himself in his mad pursuit of the monster. Although Walton, at the near-mutinous insistence of his crew, does not pursue the monster as Frankenstein wishes, the question of his future as a man and a scientist remains uncertain. Frankenstein, in spite of all that has happened to him, holds open the possibility that science and other scientists may achieve where he has failed. Thus, while he seems to be warning Walton away from the dangers he has experienced and the punishment he has suffered, he ambiguously holds out the 'carrot' of further exploration.

Frankenstein and Elizabeth

The striking contrasts between Elizabeth and Frankenstein make their pairing very important, as brother and adoptive 'sister', as an engaged couple, and finally in their very brief marriage. Frankenstein is a curiously incomplete character — a deeply flawed personality, he is for ever in need of the guidance of wise companions. Elizabeth is one of the most significant of these, and should be the most intimate. With her strength of character, indefatigable loyalty and endless patience, she is the perfect balance to Frankenstein's weakness and

Taking it
Further

Watch one or two of the recommended adaptations of the novel. How are the parallels between the characters portrayed?

...while Frankenstein seems to be warning Walton away from the dangers he has experienced... he ambiguously holds out the 'carrot' of further exploration

indiscipline. It is Frankenstein's tragedy, and Elizabeth's, that he never fully appreciates her worth. He persistently undervalues her goodness and wisdom, and in doing so seals their fates as individuals and as a couple. He fails to understand the importance of companionship — something that the monster never does — and as a result neglects Elizabeth. A solipsist by nature, he then misinterprets the monster's threats after the destruction of the second creature and in so doing ironically ensures the death of the person he claims to value most. *Frankenstein* emphasises the importance of balance and completeness. Elizabeth offers the perfect (and tragically spurned) completion and balance to Victor's personality.

*Pause for **Thought***

What other examples can you think of from your reading where authors deliberately pair characters for effect?

Frankenstein and Clerval

As friends from childhood, Frankenstein and Clerval offer the reader another important pairing. Both are ardent for knowledge; like Frankenstein, Clerval wishes to attend the university, but while Frankenstein's early dabblings in science go uncorrected by his indulgent father, Clerval's father will not allow him to attend. Both men have inquisitive and lively minds, and both imagine a glorious and renowned future for themselves, but Clerval, perhaps on account of the intervention of his father, is better able to regulate his desires. This becomes clear when, on finally arriving at Ingolstadt, he puts off his studies to nurse Frankenstein through his sickness in the wake of the creation of the monster. Clerval is caring, loving and devoted — characteristics that Frankenstein lacks.

Frankenstein and Justine Moritz

Both are falsely accused of committing a murder perpetrated by the monster. Through this parallel in their stories she becomes a measure of Frankenstein's conscience, a symbol of the destruction of innocence he has caused. She is innocent where he is (morally at least) guilty. Her death and his inability to prove her innocence (and unwillingness even to try) point to the very heart of Frankenstein's nature and the terrible dilemma he faces.

Elizabeth and Walton

Walton, like Elizabeth, has an early love of poetry, a characteristic both share with Clerval and the monster. This love of the redeeming arts, in the face of destructive science, suggests a source of hope in Walton's character. Both are closely bound to Frankenstein — Elizabeth as his 'other half' and Walton as a 'kindred spirit'.

Walton and the monster

The monster, a present reality for Frankenstein, is an imminent possibility for Walton. If the monster is a symbol of the fruits of irresponsible scientific exploration, then he is as much a part of Walton's make-up as he is of Frankenstein's. It is worth observing that Walton sights the monster before he meets Frankenstein, significantly suggesting the presence of the monster in him before Frankenstein arrives to offer an explanation.

Clerval and Elizabeth

Both Elizabeth and Clerval are poetry lovers, a characteristic which seems to indicate a civilising influence within the novel. Both suffer extremely because of their love for Frankenstein, showing the greatest personal dedication and even sacrifice for his sake. Both also seek to regulate Frankenstein's nature, with an equal lack of success.

Elizabeth and the monster's destroyed companion

Clear and significant parallels exist here. Elizabeth, as Frankenstein's bride, is obviously comparable with the potential 'bride' of the monster. Likewise, when Frankenstein destroys the monster's companion, to balance the narrative and to complete the parallels between the monster and his creator, Elizabeth must suffer the same fate as the monster's 'bride'. Although they contrast on the surface (Elizabeth a picture of beauty and the monster's companion likely to be as ugly as the monster), they come together to symbolise the importance of companionship, whether given or taken away.

The role of women

Gothic women

The connection between women and Gothic is interesting. Many of the foremost authors working in the genre have been women. Shelley, Radcliffe, Charlotte Dacre and Sophia Lee were all early Gothic authors and were very influential in the development of the form. Female characters also have a central role to play — they are frequently the victims of male domination and cruelty. At the same time, however, even where they fulfil the typical role of the victim, they often demonstrate great resilience and strength of character, surviving through the harshest

of circumstances. Gothic can thus be seen as an important vehicle for considering societal views of women.

Frankenstein deals extensively with issues of oppression and presents strong women living in the face of brutality and adversity. We need to consider how far Shelley's women are conventional Gothic figures. The women in the text all play significant and powerful roles. Even such seemingly peripheral figures as Justine Moritz, Safie and Mrs Saville force us to reconsider our expectations. Shelley's presentation of them is far from straightforward or conventional.

The majority of her female characters draw on elements of the traditional Gothic female. However, they are not stereotypically weak women, as in the works of Radcliffe, Lewis and others. Shelley's women often exert influence over the male characters. Women are a powerful driving force in the lives of Frankenstein, Frankenstein's father, Felix De Lacey and the monster, often demonstrating restraint and wisdom that the males do not. Shelley's representation of males and females therefore moves towards an equalisation of the genders, recognising the need for balance. Usually in Gothic fiction, women are seen as passive and helpless victims, while men are strong and self-reliant. The threats to women within the novel are clear, but so are the threats to the men. Clerval, William, Frankenstein's father and Frankenstein himself all fall victim to the monster.

Margaret Saville

Margaret Saville is Robert Walton's sister and correspondent (interestingly, she shares the same initials as the author of the text, Mary Shelley). As such she is a receptacle, but not an active player in the novel, and to that extent she is passive. She is an outsider to the events of the novel, and her responses are not even presented to the reader, but she holds in relation to Walton a similar position to that held by Elizabeth to Frankenstein: she is cast in the light of the absent mother figure who must remain at home awaiting news of the fate of her beloved.

Elizabeth

Elizabeth, like Mrs Saville, spends much time waiting at home for Frankenstein's correspondence. As he does with the rest of his family, Frankenstein leaves Elizabeth helpless in the face of his desertion. She is not, however, generally passive; she takes an active, if unfruitful, part in trying to save Justine Moritz when she is wrongly imprisoned for the murder of William. She is a strong character, coping with the repeated griefs inflicted on her by Frankenstein and the other events of her life.

She is, however, to some extent cast in the light of the Gothic female victim, both of the monster and of Frankenstein.

Frankenstein's mother

Frankenstein's mother is only present in memory in the novel. Frankenstein idealises her as the perfection of womanly domestic virtue. She is a strong presence in the Frankenstein household and exercises a profound influence on Frankenstein's behaviour and decisions. The power she exerts is exemplified when she (alongside Elizabeth) appears to the haunted Frankenstein in his midnight wanderings in the streets of Ingolstadt.

Safie

Safie is described as a woman of 'angelic beauty and expression'; she is the object of Felix's delight and an image of perfection. Her background, like Shelley's own, incorporates radical elements: she is taught by her mother, contrary to Islamic norms of the time, 'to aspire to higher powers of intellect and an independence of spirit forbidden to the female followers of Mahomet' (p. 127). In terms of the limits society imposes on her freedom, the reader may question whether her position is really very different from the Christian women in the novel. She has the courage to act on her own convictions, running away from her father and travelling independently to rejoin Felix.

Justine Moritz

Justine Moritz demonstrates great determination and moral strength in the face of extreme difficulties and injustice.

Agatha De Lacey

Agatha De Lacey is perhaps the most stereotypically Gothic of all the female characters. She appears as innocent and weak, depending heavily on Felix to look after her, unlike the other women in the text who are more independent.

The monster's companion

The monster's companion plays a highly significant role within the novel, even though she never actually comes into being. During her creation, Frankenstein reflects upon what the nature of the beast might be. Notice how he imagines the new monster to be a thinking, independent being, capable of making her own decisions and sticking by them in the face of

the promises of the monster. She is envisaged as possessing strength and determination of character which may threaten and override the 'authority' of the male. Frankenstein fears this.

Outsiders

The outsider is a classic figure of Gothic fiction, representing:

- the unknown
- the unacceptable
- the damned
- the fearsome
- the horrific

Mythical figures such as the Wandering Jew, the vampire and Frankenstein's monster are central to both literary and popular tradition.

All of Shelley's major characters are outsiders — disenfranchisement, disempowerment, loss of identity, loss of cohesion, loss of relationships and the destruction of familial and societal ties are all significant contributing factors.

Frankenstein

Victor Frankenstein, largely through his own fault, is isolated in his own family, then at the university, and finally left alone in the world. His choice to isolate himself from his loving and protective family is both surprising and ominous. The contrast between domestic security and extreme isolation is stark and heightens his personal tragedy. The monster reduces him to the ultimate life of the outsider, chasing backwards and forwards across Europe, with no security and no hope of refuge. He is an outsider within the natural world, separated from the beauty of godly creation; he is an outsider separated from his creator by means of his own presumptuous desires and rebellion. In transgressing acceptable boundaries, Frankenstein suffers psychological and societal exclusion.

The monster

Human society will not accommodate the monster because of his looks; people reject him on the assumption that his character is reflected in his features. His rejection by Frankenstein, his creator, serves only to compound his sense of isolation. His life in the hovel next to the De Laceys' loving and caring home captures the pathos of his situation as he desperately seeks to fit into the world around him. He is isolated from his creator and from the rest of creation by the absolute will of Frankenstein, and is therefore condemned to a life outside the bounds of society. Realising that the conventional happiness of human existence and companionship are not to be his, the monster offers to live voluntarily as an outsider in the wilds of South America if Frankenstein will create him a mate, but is further isolated when Frankenstein destroys the companion he has been creating for the monster.

Safie's father

Safie's father is an outcast in Parisian society simply because he is a foreigner. He goes on to alienate himself from his own daughter by his ungrateful and churlish betrayal of the De Laceys.

Safie

Safie shares her father's isolation in Paris. As a Muslim woman, Shelley explores her lack of rights. When her father betrays the De Laceys, she finds herself separated from her own flesh and blood, preferring to risk all in the attempt to find Felix.

Walton

Walton is isolated from his family and from the security of home by his travels. Like Frankenstein, he is a self-imposed outsider, burning with ambitious desire. On board ship he is isolated from the crew by his position as captain and by his desire to press on towards the pole, even in the face of the most extreme danger. He recognises his lack of a good companion and the potential dangers of this.

Clerval

Clerval is marginalised in Frankenstein's affections during the creation of the monster and is again distanced from him, in spite of his great loyalty, on their trip to England. Clerval's desire to go to university is opposed by his father, but unlike Frankenstein, Clerval resolves the difficulty and does not alienate himself from those he loves.

Photos12/Alamy

Boris Karloff as the monster in the classic 1931 film version

Mrs Saville

Mrs Saville is an outsider who is given no voice. She is simply the intended recipient of Walton's correspondence. This correspondence, owing to Walton's being on a ship, can only be one-sided, and as such is scarcely a correspondence at all. As Walton is Frankenstein's sole audience, so Mrs Saville is Walton's.

Elizabeth

Elizabeth is an orphan — an archetypal outsider figure. She gains the love and acceptance of the family, but is increasingly marginalised in Frankenstein's affections by his studies. Her acceptance (like Justine Moritz's) in the Frankenstein household contrasts starkly with her treatment at Victor's hands.

Frankenstein's father

Frankenstein's father is profoundly changed by the death of his wife. This is further aggravated by the way Frankenstein shuts him out of his confidence when he goes to Ingolstadt. As his family members are killed one by one at the hands of the monster, he is more and more acutely isolated, until at last he pines away.

Justine Moritz

Like Elizabeth, Justine is an orphan. She becomes an outsider to society when charged with William's murder, although she never loses the faith of her adoptive family.

The De Laceys

The De Laceys lose both social position and wealth when they courageously support Safie's father in the face of popular prejudice. When Safie's father treacherously betrays them, they are forced to flee Paris and to live a humble and lonely life in Switzerland, a situation exacerbated by their poverty.

Form, structure and language

Form

Other information relating to form, structure and language can be found throughout this book. Detailed information about the Gothic form within which the novel operates can be found on pp. 59–61 of this guide. The *Themes* section also looks closely at issues of form, structure and language relating to Shelley's use of the elements, nature, dreams and the supernatural.

About the novel

The idea for Shelley's most celebrated novel came during a summer stay with her husband, Byron and Polidori at the Villa Diodati by Lake Geneva in Switzerland, very near to Victor Frankenstein's home town. At Byron's suggestion they each told a ghost story. Shelley told the first version of what was to become *Frankenstein*. It was first published anonymously in 1818 in three-volume form, when Shelley was only 20, followed by a two-volume edition, bearing the author's name (1823), and a revised single-volume version (1831). Deeply concerned with social issues, the novel carries the unmistakable imprint of Shelley's parents, Mary Wollstonecraft and William Godwin. Wollstonecraft is recognised as one of the great early champions of female rights, expounded in works such as *Maria* and *A Vindication of the Rights of Women*, while Godwin was both novelist (*The Adventures of Caleb Williams, Mandeville* and *Fleetwood*) and political thinker (*Enquiry Concerning the Principles of Political Justice*). The novel is also heavily influenced by the Romantics (especially Wordsworth, Coleridge and Percy Bysshe Shelley), and Milton's *Paradise Lost*. Another major formal influence is the canon of Gothic fiction; we know from Shelley's journal that she had read Radcliffe, Lewis (who visited the party at the Villa Diodati), Charles Robert Maturin and William Beckford, all central figures in the Gothic movement.

...the novel carries the unmistakable imprint of Shelley's parents, Mary Wollstonecraft and William Godwin

The three-volume novel

The three-volume novel was a major stage in the development of the modern novel and became a standard publishing format in nineteenth-century England. It does not correspond to current ideas of a trilogy of novels, which are three related yet distinct works of fiction. Instead it was the publication of a single work in three sections or instalments. This was economically driven. Books were relatively expensive to print and purchase, so a system had to be devised to maintain the developing publishing industry. A novel divided into three parts could create a demand (Part I whetting an appetite for Parts II and III); in addition, the income from Part I could pay for the printing costs of the later parts. The form became particularly successful in mid-Victorian times when it became closely related to the work of the circulating libraries.

The price of each volume remained stable at half a guinea for most of the nineteenth century — roughly equivalent to the cost of a high-quality hardback book today (around £20). The cost of a single novel, in other words, was one and a half guineas (approximately £60). Around two-thirds of novels first published in book form (not already serialised in magazines) were released as three-volume sets; reprints of successful three-volume novels were often done in cheap one-volume editions.

Task *10*

The following typical elements of science fiction are present in *Frankenstein*. Explore the details of each:

- grotesque monsters and aliens
- fear of the outsider, the foreign and the alien
- flawed scientific experiment and its consequences
- threat to established society
- use of 'cutting edge' or invented technology
- the character of the 'mad scientist'

Multiple narratives

The use of multiple narrators is typical of Gothic fiction. Classic genre texts such as *The Monk* (Lewis), *Melmoth the Wanderer* (Maturin) and *Dracula* (Stoker) all employ the device. It is also used to considerable effect in *Frankenstein*. We need to consider why Shelley chose this method, and its impact. The testimony of various narrators could be a method to add plausibility to a tale which otherwise lacks verisimilitude (truth to life). It also provides a range of perceptions of and responses to events, allowing us a more rounded view of what occurs. But in *Frankenstein*, the device goes further than this. The connected narratives grow organically from one another: it is impossible to extricate them one from the other — the monster's narrative is part of Frankenstein's narrative and vice versa. Similarly, Frankenstein's narrative is subsumed within that of Walton.

Science fiction

While the actual form of science fiction as we know it today did not really emerge until some time later (Jules Verne's 1864 novel *Journey to the Centre of the Earth* and H. G. Wells's *The Time Machine* of 1895 being key early examples), Shelley's novel clearly has strong claims to be the first great science fiction novel. In its focus on dystopian possibilities, the heroic fantasy of the hero, its reliance on horror, the paranormal and scientific advance, it contains a wealth of the ingredients that define the science fiction genre.

Structure

The shape of the narrative

First consider the sequence of the narrative: Walton — Frankenstein — Monster — Frankenstein — Walton. The narrative might thus be perceived and interpreted in a number of ways.

V-shaped

Walton   **Walton**
        Frankenstein   **Frankenstein**
                        Monster

This suggests that Walton's narrative is the surface of the novel's events — it is the narrative 'present' with which the novel begins and ends. Below that surface lies Victor Frankenstein's tale — a cautionary tale relating to Walton's potential future. At the 'deepest' point of the tale lies the monster's narrative, embodying the deepest and darkest psychological forces of the novel. The V may thus suggest a descent into darkness and re-emergence from it. The open V also suggests an open-ended conclusion to the tale. We are left uncertain as to the monster's fate (has he indeed gone to his death at the North Pole?), and we are also uncertain of Walton's future. Frankenstein's highly ambiguous closing observations on scientific exploration leave us doubting whether Walton will heed the warning he has received.

Chinese boxes

This implies a new relationship between the narratives. Unlike the open-ended possibilities of the V shape, this view suggests a closed ending to the novel. Walton's tale, the frame narrative of the novel, encloses the narrative of Victor Frankenstein. The close parallels between the two men suggest close links between their narratives,

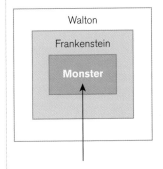

especially as Victor's narrative is scribed by Walton. The potential for Walton to become another Frankenstein adds significance to the enclosure of Victor's narrative within Walton's. Likewise, the monster's narrative is embedded within Frankenstein's. Again, this signals the inescapable ties between the two characters; as Frankenstein's creature, the monster's narrative cannot be read as distinct from Frankenstein's and vice versa.

Tellingly, the monster's narrative lies at the heart of the tale — to borrow a phrase from Joseph Conrad, it is the novel's 'heart of darkness', without which neither Frankenstein's nor Walton's narratives can stand. The concept of boxes also relates to Prometheus, who is sometimes linked to Pandora, from whose box emerged untold horrors. The monster can be seen as the forbidden 'box' at the heart of Shelley's tale, which Frankenstein foolishly opens, allowing horror and turmoil to spill out into the world.

Concentric rings

As in the previous model, the monster's narrative is completely enclosed within Frankenstein's, which is enclosed within Walton's frame story. Again, this emphasises the inescapable interrelations and interactions between all three narratives and points to the monster as the core of *Frankenstein*. The rings, however, suggest a different direction in the narrative. Whereas the 'V' implies a linear movement through the novel, and the boxes imply a movement inwards from Walton through Frankenstein to the monster, this model implies a movement outwards from the monster, making him the driving force of the novel. The narratives are like a set of spreading rings on water. Walton's first sighting of the monster comes before he has even met Frankenstein, and therefore we see that the monster precedes Victor in Walton's imagination; it is the monster that drives Frankenstein's insane pursuit and fuels his desire for revenge; and it is the 'monster' of scientific ambition in Frankenstein that leads to the sorry events we see.

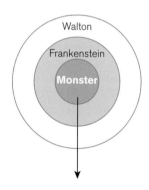

Linked narratives and narrators

Shelley links her three narratives closely, suggesting the significant connections between the tellers and their tales. These connections and parallels are explored extensively in the 'Pairings' section on pp. 30–33 of this guide. So detailed are the parallels between the lives of Walton, Frankenstein and the monster that we see their existences as integrally related. Indeed, in the case of the monster and Victor, the distinctions

PHILIP ALLAN LITERATURE GUIDE **FOR A-LEVEL**

between them become increasingly blurred until they can arguably be perceived as one — in the popular imagination, Frankenstein is often taken to be the name of the monster.

The close linking of Frankenstein and Walton is also highly significant, as it emphasises the danger Walton faces if he continues with his current course and attitudes. Victor also acts as a bridge between the monster and Walton. The monster is at the heart of both Frankenstein and Walton, encouraging a symbolic reading of their relationship — Shelley establishes an unholy trinity: rather than the biblical trinity of God the Father, the Son and the Holy Spirit, we have the father (Frankenstein), the son (Walton) and the unholy spirit (the monster).

Doubling of plot devices

It is not only in her use of characters that Shelley employs the device of doubling. Throughout the novel she doubles plot devices. This links to one of the great features of Gothic fiction — cyclical repetition. Through repetition and mutation, the way in which Shelley structures the text ensures that the tale has an inevitable and inescapable logic.

Listed below are some key examples of this:

- false accusations of murder against both Justine and Frankenstein
- the dumping of the monster's companion and Clerval in the Irish Sea
- Frankenstein's scientific exploration and Walton's scientific voyage
- the monster's rejection by society and the De Laceys' rejection
- the destruction of the monster's companion and of Elizabeth
- the traitorous betrayal of the monster by Frankenstein and the betrayal of the De Laceys by Safie's father
- the novel's doubling of plot elements from *The Rime of the Ancient Mariner*, *Paradise Lost* and the Prometheus myth

Task 11

Consider the list of doubled plot devices and add any others you can think of. What effects does Shelley create through this paralleled structure of events?

Paradise Lost and The Rime of the Ancient Mariner

These two great poems by Milton and Coleridge are both very significant in understanding *Frankenstein*. The plot structure of the novel is closely linked to the narrative of the poems, and at times the characters in Shelley's tale find themselves acting according to the dictates of these literary models.

Paradise Lost

Paradise Lost is one of the books the monster reads, and it powerfully influences his view of the world, but it is also a formative influence on the narrative as a whole. It is based on the story of Adam and Eve from Genesis. The poem tells of their creation, disobedience and consequent banishment from Paradise. It also tells the story of Satan, an angel who leads an attempted rebellion against God, and who is punished by being sent to hell. As an act of revenge against God, he causes the Fall of mankind by tempting Eve in the form of the serpent.

A number of detailed structural comparisons with *Frankenstein* are important. Like the devils after their failed rebellion against God, the monster is forced to forge a life for himself away from his creator (Book 1) and eventually seeks to avenge himself on his creator by attacking his most beloved (Book 2). Like Satan, the monster undertakes long, perilous journeys to fulfil his schemes (Book 3), resolving in the exact terms the monster uses ('Evil be thou my Good') to have his way. He is jealous because he can never possess the Paradise that Adam and Eve inhabit (Book 4). Frankenstein receives warnings from his father about his dangerous behaviour in the same way that Adam and Eve do from the angel Raphael (Book 5). Adam tells of his loneliness and his request for God to create him a companion, a situation which relates closely to the monster's (Book 8). After they fall to Satan's temptation, Adam and Eve fall into despair, aware that their disobedience has separated them from God — this is similar to Frankenstein's experience. Satan and the monster both gain their revenge (Book 9). Adam and Eve recognise what they have done and resolve to seek mercy (Book 10). By contrast, Frankenstein determines to pursue his own revenge on the monster, but in both texts the central characters are banished from Paradise because of their actions (Book 11).

The Rime of the Ancient Mariner

Structural influences also exist between *Frankenstein* and *The Rime of the Ancient Mariner*. Walton, like the wedding guest, is accosted by a mentally unstable stranger who forces him to listen to his cautionary tale. Polar regions are significant in both tales, and both tale-tellers live in fear of their actions (Part 1). The mariner's ship, like Walton's, becomes dangerously entrapped in the ice, and the mariner himself, like Frankenstein, becomes an outcast because of his actions (Part 2). Death visits the ship, taking the mariner's companions from him one by one, as Victor's family circle is removed from him by the monster (Part 3). The mariner cannot pray — a characteristic he shares with Victor — but at last, unlike Frankenstein, he is able to thank God and is released from his burden (Part 4). The becalmed ship is now able to move again and sails clear, as Walton is able to do once Frankenstein has died, and returns homeward (Parts 5 and 6). The mariner, like Frankenstein, is tormented by his experiences, which he is compelled to tell. The tale has an impact on the wedding guest, who returns to the feast 'a sadder and wiser man'. The influence of Frankenstein's tale on Walton is less clear.

Taking it Further ▶

Find Gustave Doré's illustrations for *The Rime of the Ancient Mariner* using an internet search engine such as Google Images. Compare their settings and atmosphere to Walton's narrative. (One is on p. 64 of this guide.)

Language

Verbal ties — Victor and the monster

At a number of points in the novel, Shelley creates verbal ties between Frankenstein and the monster. Through such verbal echoes, Shelley emphasises the connections between creator and creature:

- The monster: 'I, like the archfiend, bore a hell within me' (p. 138). Compare this to Frankenstein's: 'I was cursed by some devil, and carried about with me my eternal hell' (p. 207).

- Shelley tellingly makes use of the word 'consummate' with regard to Frankenstein's wedding night — it is to be the night that the monster consummates his crime, as well as the night that Frankenstein and Elizabeth consummate their marriage. The double meaning in the word alerts us to two further 'marriages' — the marriage of death between the monster and Elizabeth (a direct act of revenge mirroring Frankenstein's destruction of the monster's companion) and the marriage of Frankenstein and his monster in deadly pursuit.

- Compare Frankenstein's: 'I would sell my life dearly, and not shrink from the conflict until my own life, or that of my adversary, was extinguished' (p. 198) to the monster's: 'you, my creator, detest and spurn me, thy creature, to whom thou art bound by ties only dissoluble by the annihilation of one of us' (p. 102).

Shelley's use of this technique establishes the intimate connection between Frankenstein and his monster. Even though they are in many ways extremely isolated one from the other, Shelley uses verbal ties to emphasise the inescapable connections between the creator and his creature. Unconsciously, they think and speak in the same terms.

Biblical imagery

Biblical imagery lies at the heart of one of the key source texts for the novel, *Paradise Lost* (see pp. 43–44 of this guide). Shelley's use of biblical imagery and language, however, plays an important role in its own right. First note the nature of Shelley's tale of creation (Genesis) and apocalypse (Revelation) — the first and last books of the Bible. A number of key ideas from Genesis are significant:

- the story of God's creation
- the particular emphasis on the relationship between God and humanity
- the instruction for humanity to multiply and 'subdue' the world
- the temptation to challenge God's authority
- sin and the Fall of humanity
- banishment from the Garden of Eden
- the murderous relationship between Cain and Abel, the sons of Adam and Eve

The books of Revelation (sometimes called 'The Apocalypse') and Daniel are also significant, as examples of apocalyptic literature — literature that deals with events at the end of time:

- the concept of judgement
- war, death and destruction
- strange composite beasts
- the wrath of God against sinful humanity
- the promise of a coming heavenly state
- the battle between good and evil

Task 12

Make notes explaining how each of the ideas from the Bible listed relates to *Frankenstein*.

Frankenstein can also be seen as prophetic, a kind of wisdom literature. While she is not didactic in approaching her subject, Shelley has clear moral intentions. The words of the monster to his creator on the 'sea of ice' and elsewhere have the weighty tone of the prophetic books of the Old Testament. The monster, like the Old Testament prophets, warns Frankenstein starkly of how he should behave. He offers him alternatives, one of which will lead to redemption, while the other must lead to death and destruction for one or both of them. Frankenstein ironically comes to see himself as humanity's only potential saviour, but in seeking to destroy the monster and to prevent the furtherance of his species by refusing to create a companion, he seals his own fate. Redemption and salvation, such central principles of the biblical message, play a very different role in *Frankenstein*.

Language of heaven and hell

Gothic often makes use of opposites and contrasts. The ultimate contrast in Christian tradition is between heaven, the perfection of union with God, and hell, the eternal torment of separation from God. Shelley frequently employs the language of heaven and hell in the course of the novel. Frankenstein often uses hellish language in referring to the monster — 'the fiend', 'diabolical'. Almost by way of compensation, he uses heavenly language in the context of his mother and Elizabeth, who represent for him (in terms of their femininity, their caring natures, their love and their beauty) everything that he will not allow the monster to be.

Task 13

Find a selection of examples of Shelley's use of the language of heaven and hell. Analyse their effect.

Contexts

Biographical context

1797 30 August, Mary Godwin is born to William Godwin and Mary Wollstonecraft; mother dies ten days later.

1812 Percy Bysshe Shelley pays regular visits to Godwin and meets Mary.

1814 Mary begins a relationship with the married Shelley.

1815 Gives birth to a daughter, who dies shortly afterwards.

1816 Gives birth to a son; moves to Geneva; Shelley's wife drowns; he marries Mary.

1817 *Frankenstein* completed.

1818 *Frankenstein* published.

1819 Semi-autobiographical novel *Mathilda* written.

1822 Percy Bysshe Shelley dies, lost at sea.

1824 Mary publishes her husband's *Posthumous Poems*.

1836 William Godwin dies.

1851 1 February, Mary dies in London.

Biographical sketch

Mary Shelley was born on 30 August 1797, in London. She came from a fertile and radical literary background. Her father was William Godwin, an influential political theorist, novelist and publisher; he encouraged her early attempts as a writer. Her mother, Mary Wollstonecraft, was also a writer and a significant early feminist thinker. Sadly, she died of puerperal fever only ten days after Mary's birth. As a child, Mary was introduced to many of her father's intellectual circle, including William Hazlitt (critic), Charles Lamb (essayist) and Samuel Taylor Coleridge (poet). She also met the great Romantic poet Percy Bysshe Shelley in 1812, when she was 15. Although married at the time, Shelley took Mary travelling in the summer of 1814. Mary fell pregnant and had a premature baby girl early in 1815. The child died 12 days later. Mary's journal for 19 March 1815 reads: 'Dream that my little baby came to life again — that it had only been cold & that we rubbed it before the fire & it lived.' It is tempting to see in this poignant moment of personal tragedy the genesis of her ideas for *Frankenstein*. William, their son, was born in January 1816. They were married in December 1816, soon after Harriet (Shelley's first wife) drowned. Another daughter, Clara, was born in 1817, but she survived only one year.

Frankenstein, published in 1818 when Mary was 21, was a huge success. Her husband wrote an anonymous preface, but many refused to believe such a tale could have been written by a young woman, and attributed it to her husband. In the same year, the Shelleys left England for Italy where, following the death of their son William at the age of three, Mary suffered a nervous breakdown. Only Percy Florence, born in 1819, survived past childhood, but death still stalked Mary: her husband drowned during a heavy squall in the Gulf of Spezia in 1822. At the young age of 25 and a widow, she returned to England with her son and continued her career as a professional writer. Shelley gave up writing long fiction when Victorian realism started to gain popularity, but continued to write numerous short stories for periodicals and produced several volumes of lives for Dionysius Lardner's *Cabinet Cyclopedia* and the first authoritative edition of Percy Bysshe Shelley's poems (1839, 4 vols.). She died from a brain tumour in Bournemouth on 1 February 1851 at the age of 54.

Mary Wollstonecraft and William Godwin

Mary Shelley's parents were both significant figures in the literary and political world. Her mother, Mary Wollstonecraft, was of unconventional beliefs, part of the Rational Dissenters sect, who did not believe in original sin and eternal punishment. She also became associated with radical politics and began to form her progressive views on women's rights, publishing *Thoughts on the Education of Girls* in 1786. Her minister, Richard Price, supported the French Revolution and argued that the British, like the French, had the right to remove a bad king from the throne. When Edmund Burke attacked Price, Wollstonecraft wrote *A Vindication of the Rights of Man* in his defence, demonstrating her powerful and progressive political views on the topic of revolution, the evils of society, the slave trade, game laws and the

treatment of the poor. This brought her to the attention of other major radical figures such as Thomas Paine, Godwin and William Blake, several of whom she met.

In *A Vindication of the Rights of Women*, Wollstonecraft attacked the 'ignorance and slavish dependence' in which many women were trapped because of educational restrictions, attacked society's demand that women be 'docile and attentive to their looks to the exclusion of all else', and labelled marriage as 'legal prostitution'. Needless to say, these were revolutionary and controversial ideas. One critic dubbed her 'a hyena in petticoats'. She went further, arguing that England needed to rid itself of the monarchy, the church and military hierarchies if it were to attain a state of social equality. Within this she formed her feminist creed, advocating female suffrage.

In 1793 she moved to France with the American writer, Gilbert Imlay, but this relationship did not last, and she returned to England where she married William Godwin in 1797. Soon afterwards she gave birth to her daughter Mary, but died from blood poisoning on 10 September 1797.

William Godwin trained for a career as a dissenting minister but, plagued by doubts, gave up his vocation after less than four years, declaring himself a 'complete unbeliever'. In 1793 he published his most famous work, *An Enquiry Concerning Political Justice*, closely followed by his best novel, *Caleb Williams*. He believed that governments limited individuality and personal integrity, and he propounded a form of personal anarchism. These books deeply affected several of the major Romantics, including Wordsworth, Coleridge and Percy Bysshe Shelley, and nearly led to prosecution.

*Pause for **Thought***

How do these biographical details about Mary Shelley's parents relate to *Frankenstein*?

After Godwin became the lover of Mary Wollstonecraft and married her, he was grief-stricken at her death shortly afterwards. It was not until four years later that he was married again, to Mary Jane Clairmont, a successful publisher of children's books. Godwin wrote several children's books as well as other novels — *St Leon* and *Fleetwood*. The household frequently hosted literary and political guests, who shaped the education of the children, including the young Mary. In 1812, Percy Bysshe Shelley, a precocious poet and intellectual, became a frequent visitor at the Godwins. His marriage was collapsing and he developed a warm attachment to Mary. At the age of only 16, she ran away with the still married poet, and even though a political radical, Godwin struggled with this unconventional state of affairs. He never again enjoyed an easy relationship with either his daughter or her poet husband, although he is the dedicatee of *Frankenstein* and acted as Mary's literary agent.

He continued to write himself, producing biographies (including a life of Chaucer), plays, political works (*Of Population* and *History of the Commonwealth of England*), novels (*Mandeville, Cloudesley* and *Deloraine*), and philosophy (*Thoughts on Man*). He died in April 1836.

Coming from this free-thinking and radical background, it is easy to see the conditions under which the precociously talented Mary developed, and to understand the ferment of ideas from which *Frankenstein*, her first and most famous novel, emerged.

The writing of *Frankenstein*

In May 1816, Mary Godwin, Percy Bysshe Shelley and their son William travelled to Geneva to meet Byron, who was renting the Villa Diodati at Cologny, near the shores of Lac Leman. They spent the summer there. Other guests included Byron's personal physician, John Polidori, and other occasional visitors, such as the Gothic novelist Matthew 'Monk' Lewis. Percy Bysshe Shelley and Mary did not in fact stay at the Villa Diodati, but at the Maison Chapuis on the waterfront nearby. Typically their days comprised writing, boating on the lake, and talking late into the night.

Recalling that summer in 1831, Mary wrote: 'It proved a wet, ungenial summer, and incessant rain often confined us for days to the house.' In the long conversations this enforced, they talked at length amongst other things about the experiments of the eighteenth-century natural philosopher and poet Erasmus Darwin, who was said to have brought dead matter to life. They also spoke about the experiments of the Italian scientist Luigi Galvani and of the feasibility of returning a corpse or assembled body parts to life. German ghost stories, read around the log fire at the Villa Diodati, provided another form of entertainment, and this prompted Byron to suggest they each write their own tale of the supernatural. Shortly afterwards, in a waking dream, Mary Godwin conceived the idea for *Frankenstein*:

> **I saw the pale student of unhallowed arts kneeling beside the thing he had put together. I saw the hideous phantasm of a man stretched out, and then, on the working of some powerful engine, show signs of life, and stir with an uneasy, half vital motion. Frightful must it be; for supremely frightful would be the effect of any human endeavour to mock the stupendous mechanism of the Creator of the world.**

With her husband's encouragement, she began writing the tale that was to become her first novel, *Frankenstein*. She was later to describe that

Taking it
Further

Do an internet search to find out about Erasmus Darwin and Luigi Galvani.

'…supremely frightful would be the effect of any human endeavour to mock the stupendous mechanism of the Creator'

summer in Switzerland as the moment 'when I first stepped out from childhood into life'.

Historical context

Revolution

Shelley's life was marked at its beginning and its end by revolution. At the beginning of her life, the *fin-de-siècle* eighteenth-century world was turned upside down by major revolutions on either side of the Atlantic: the French Revolution (1789) and the American Revolution (1775). A further wave of revolutions then swept across Europe in 1848 near the end of her life. *Frankenstein* was written against this background of revolution, and the excitement and fear that went with it.

The French Revolution began in July 1789 with the storming of the infamous Bastille prison. In October, King Louis XVI and his family were removed from their palace at Versailles and his powers were ceded to a Legislative Assembly. Louis was tried by a newly proclaimed Republic in December 1792, and executed in January 1793. The Republic then declared war on England, a state of affairs that would last for a further 22 years. After the execution of the king, the Reign of Terror began — Robespierre's ruthless extermination of potential enemies, regardless of gender, age or condition. In the last six weeks of the Terror in Paris alone (late June and July 1794), almost 1,400 people were guillotined. A succession of revolutionary governments led to the eventual proclamation of Napoleon Bonaparte as emperor in 1804.

All of this had a profound influence on English intellectual, philosophical and political life. At first it was seen as a triumph of reason over superstition and privilege, and was welcomed by English radicals like Paine, Blake and Shelley's father, William Godwin. They read the initial revolution as a symbolic act presaging the return of a state of perfection from which humanity had fallen away. As the revolution descended into the excesses of the Terror, however, initial enthusiasm turned to disillusionment.

The fear of unknown powers (especially the power of the common people) was rife among the ruling and privileged classes in Britain, who had seen their French counterparts toppled and the country subjected to the Terror. The unleashing of these powers, accompanying (and in many ways related to) the burgeoning industrial revolution with all its scientific

As the revolution descended into the excesses of the Terror... initial enthusiasm turned to disillusionment

*Pause for **Thought***

What parallels can you detect between these historical events and the events of the novel?

advances, manufacturing changes, travel possibilities and societal change, created deep fears and unease within the establishment.

All of this reflects interestingly on Shelley's novel. The actions of Frankenstein and Walton can be closely related to the scientific, technological and exploratory advances of the time — their own kind of revolution. Frankenstein, in particular, challenges accepted societal norms and transgresses boundaries established by conventional religious belief. The monster, therefore, can be seen as the dark potential powers that these 'revolutions' unleash. The violence the monster wreaks on Frankenstein and his family calls to mind the violence of revolutionary France, where the unchecked, selfish actions of the aristocracy were turned on their heads in the brutal finality of Robespierre and the revolutionaries.

The 'Peterloo Massacre'

In England, fear of revolution was very real. War against Napoleon's France had been going on for more than 20 years. In addition, the nature of the land was changing with the industrial revolution. The trend towards urbanisation, which would peak in the latter decades of the nineteenth century, and which would see the growth of the great industrial urban centres of the Midlands and the north of England, was already under way. With these changes came new demands for more equitable representation within the political system, which represented only the interests and voices of the privileged few. The franchise movement had begun, calling for reform of the electoral system (major Reform Acts would be passed in 1832, 1867 and 1884).

In March 1819 the Manchester Patriotic Union Society was formed. It attracted all of Manchester's leading radicals. Its main objective was to achieve reform of Parliament, and in the summer of 1819 several well-known orators were invited to speak at a public meeting to be held at St Peter's Field in Manchester. Local magistrates, concerned that this would be a very large meeting and that the would-be reformers might spark a riot, arranged for a large number of soldiers to be in Manchester on the day of the meeting. The force comprised approximately a thousand cavalry, several hundred infantrymen, a detachment of the Royal Horse Artillery, two six-pounder guns and 400 special constables.

At about 11 o'clock on the morning of 16 August, the magistrates met at a house overlooking St Peter's Field. The meeting proceeded peacefully, but they became concerned at the rapid growth of the crowd — estimates of the number present vary, but it is likely that there were

at least 50,000 people present by midday. The magistrates sent in the special constables to clear a path through the crowd to the hustings.

The main speakers — Henry Hunt, Richard Carlile and others — arrived at 1.20 p.m. They were joined on the platform by several members of the press. At 1.30 p.m. the magistrates decided that the gathering now represented a significant threat to the city and instructed the deputy constable to arrest Hunt and the other leaders of the demonstration. The deputy constable insisted that he needed military assistance. The magistrates concurred and wrote orders. The Manchester and Salford Yeomanry, commanded by Major Trafford, entered St Peter's Field along the path cleared by the special constables. Their behaviour was erratic — a fact put down by some to the fear of their horses on entering such a large crowd, and by others to drink. As the soldiers approached the hustings, people in the crowd realised what was happening, linked arms and broke through the pathway created by the special constables to prevent them arresting the speakers. Some of the soldiers drew their sabres and began to cut their way through the crowd. When they managed to reach the hustings, eight men including Hunt were arrested. Members of the press were also detained.

*Pause for **Thought***

What 'monsters' do you see at work in this account of the events at St Peter's Field?

At 1.50 p.m. the magistrates, convinced the crowd was attacking the soldiers, ordered Lieutenant Colonel L'Estrange to go to the rescue and to disperse the crowd. The order was duly enacted, and by 2 p.m. the soldiers had driven most of the crowd from St Peter's Field, killing 18 people and wounding about 500, including 100 women.

Carlile, one of the organisers of the meeting, managed to avoid arrest and fled to London, where he quickly spread the word about the massacre at Manchester and published an account of the events he had witnessed. For his pains, he was chased down by the authorities, had the entire stock of his Fleet Street shop confiscated and was later imprisoned for publishing the story. The Peterloo Massacre, as it came to be known, became a rallying cry for radicals and played an important part in agitating popular feeling against the authorities, which appeared as repressive and anti-democratic.

In the wake of the massacre, the authorities closed ranks against the burgeoning demand for political reform. Sidmouth, the home secretary, wrote complimenting the Manchester magistrates on their actions against the crowd, and the Six Acts were passed, banning reform meetings in future. Several of the organisers of the meeting, including Hunt, were tried and imprisoned on the charge of 'assembling with unlawful banners at an unlawful meeting for the purpose of exciting discontent'.

This was an event that scarred the political and social landscape of Britain.

Mary Shelley's husband, Percy, wrote his poem 'The Masque of Anarchy' as a direct response to the events at St Peter's Field. It is a powerful attack on what he saw as unjust forms of authority ('God, and King, and Law') and a call to a radically new form of social action.

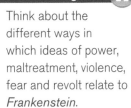

Pause for **Thought**

Think about the different ways in which ideas of power, maltreatment, violence, fear and revolt relate to *Frankenstein*.

Cultural context

Romanticism

Another significant cultural context for *Frankenstein* is Romanticism. Generally speaking, Romanticism was a late eighteenth- and early nineteenth-century movement in music, art and literature. Because of the nature of the Romantic temperament, it is hard to define. However, it emphasises:

- individual sensibility
- the boundless
- the indefinite
- the visionary

Because of its prioritisation of the individual and the relationship of humanity with numinous concepts like the visionary and the sublime, fuller definition is difficult. The *Oxford Companion to English Literature*, however, offers the following:

> **In the most abstract terms, Romanticism may be regarded as the triumph of the values of imaginative spontaneity, visionary originality, wonder, and emotional self-expression over the classical standards of order, restraint, proportion, and objectivity...Its name derives from romance, the literary form in which desires and dreams prevail over everyday realities.**

Romanticism was a profound, quasi-spiritual reaction to the confined and orderly rationalism of the Enlightenment. The Romantics asserted the importance of individual feeling, warning against the incursion of hard 'reason'. Wordsworth decried what he called the 'meddling intellect' and looked for meaning in the human heart, arguing that science, with

Pause for **Thought**

Shelley, through her marriage, was very closely associated with the Romantics. How does each of the key ideas of Romanticism relate to *Frankenstein*?

its tendency to dissect the natural world and its endless desire to define and categorise, was the negation of poetry. In Germany the philosopher Emmanuel Kant encouraged many Romantics to elevate nature, seeing in it a reflection of the soul, the sublime and the divine. Meanwhile, in France, Rousseau asserted the rights of the individual and the need for greater corporate responsibility, and in England, political thinkers like Thomas Carlyle, Godwin and Wollstonecraft wrote a new sociopolitical agenda. These revolutionary ideas led to a period of enormous social and political upheaval (including European and American revolutions).

Radicalism

The term 'radical' (from the Latin *radix*, meaning 'root') was used during the late eighteenth century for members of the Radical movement, later becoming a general term for political reformers. In the wake of the French Revolution, major figures such as Thomas Paine, Richard Price, Mary Wollstonecraft, Jeremy Bentham and William Godwin emerged. They encouraged mass support for democratic reform and rejected the aristocracy, monarchy and privilege. Some radicals sought political reform, while others championed social welfare. Popular radicals called for land nationalisation and a socialist redistribution of wealth. They also sought the right to vote, and the Corresponding Societies issued a manifesto demanding universal male suffrage and annual elections. Comparatively few people were involved with these movements, but for the first time working men were coming together to agitate for political change.

Unsurprisingly, there was a harsh backlash from the authorities, which sought to strengthen their position through legislation such as the Seditious Meetings Act (1795), which forbade impromptu large public meetings of more than 50, the highly unpopular Corn Laws (which maintained corn at unfairly high prices by punitively taxing imports of corn to England) and stern measures throughout the period of the Napoleonic Wars. William Cobbett and Henry Hunt began to press for parliamentary reform (only three men in a hundred, and no women at all, had the vote). A sequence of radical riots in 1816 and 1817 culminated in the Peterloo Massacre (see pp. 53–55 of this guide), leading to the repressive Six Acts of 1819, which further limited the right to demonstrate or hold public meetings. The powers of the magistracy were extended to help them crush demonstrations by manufacturers and action by radical Luddites, who often protested by destroying manufacturing machinery.

Given Shelley's connections through her parents with this world of political and social radicalism, this provides an important cultural context for the writing of *Frankenstein*. The plight of the repressed minority — the monster, the De Laceys and Safie — in the face of unbending society touches closely on the tenets and concerns of radicalism. The novel challenges the basis of social constructs, social distinctions and their validity.

*Pause for **Thought***

What is so radical about *Frankenstein*?

Napoleonic Wars

Although the Napoleonic Wars were a sequence of historic events, the fear engendered in the wake of the French Revolution was such that the wars were also a significant cultural event, shaping the state of the nation and impacting on the young Shelley. They were a series of conflicts fought against the French Empire, headed by Napoleon Bonaparte. Nations across Europe allied in the face of a common fear in the wake of the wars sparked by the French Revolution. The nature of warfare was revolutionised because this conflict was on an unprecedented scale. Mass conscription was used for the first time to combat rising French power as Napoleon's forces conquered most of Europe. However, the empire was to collapse rapidly after Napoleon's disastrous invasion of Russia (1812). Following the fall of the French Empire after Napoleon's defeat at Waterloo, other empires also collapsed or were substantially weakened. The Holy Roman Empire and the Spanish Empire were both seriously affected, creating a power vacuum and paving the way for British imperial expansion.

England lived in a state of fear of invasion throughout the period of the Napoleonic Wars. The characters of the novel, especially the monster, can clearly be related to these culturally momentous events, and may also be related to the imperial and colonial expansion that was only beginning at the time Shelley wrote the novel, but which was in full swing by the time she died in 1851.

Luigi Galvani

The end of the eighteenth and the beginning of the nineteenth centuries were a period of phenomenal scientific advance and provide an obvious cultural backdrop for Shelley's novel (see the section on science in *Themes*, pp. 23–27). One of the specific influences on Shelley writing the novel, however, was the Italian scientist Luigi Galvani. Working at the University of Bologna in the 1780s, he performed a series of experiments

involving electric charges and frogs. He discovered that an electric charge applied to the spinal cord of a frog could generate muscular spasms, even if the legs were no longer attached to the living frog. He became convinced that he was seeing the effects of what he called 'animal electricity'.

An eighteenth-century diagram of Galvani's experiment with frogs' legs

In one strange case, the effect was achieved when the frog's legs were in no direct contact with a source of electricity. Galvani wrote:

> **While one of those who were assisting me touched lightly, and by chance, the point of his scalpel to the internal crural nerves of the frog, suddenly all the muscles of its limbs were seen to be so contracted that they seemed to have fallen into tonic convulsions.**

In a further extract from an account of his experiments, he wrote:

> **Therefore having noticed that frog preparations which hung by copper hooks from the iron railings surrounding a balcony of our house contracted not only during thunder storms but also in fine weather, I decided to determine whether or not these contractions were due to the action of atmospheric electricity…Finally…I began to scrape and press the hook fastened to the backbone against the iron railing to see whether by such a procedure contractions might be excited, and whether instead of an alteration in the condition of the atmospheric electricity some other changes might be effective. I then noticed frequent contractions, none of which depended on variations in the weather.**

Galvani's remarkable experiments established a basis for the study of neurophysiology and neurology, and established the electrical nature of nerve–muscle function. His name lives on in the term 'galvanism'.

The direct relevance of this to *Frankenstein* is clear. Galvani, as a researcher in the field of the natural sciences, is immediately established as a counterpart to Frankenstein, obsessed with the determination to prove his theories. The links are closer than this, however. The novel's focus upon the concept of animating dead matter comes directly from the experiments of Galvani, and in both the novel and Galvani's work the presence of atmospheric electricity and lightning storms is significant.

Europe and travel

Frankenstein depends upon travel and place. Not only do the many locations provide us with a panoramic view of early nineteenth-century Europe and beyond; they also link closely to the novel's greater concerns. The powerful questions of ethics and the permissible boundaries of scientific research, the tormented psychology of Victor Frankenstein, and the tortured existence of the monster he creates are all intimately bound up with wilderness, restlessness and perpetual motion — and all this at a time when most people did not travel and when travel was a long and arduous process.

Task *14*

To gain a sense of the diversity of Shelley's locations and the distances involved, print off an outline map of Europe and plot the locations she employs:

- Russia: St Petersburg, Archangel, Black Sea
- Arctic Circle
- North Pole
- Switzerland: Lucerne, Geneva, Jura mountains, Belrive, Lausanne, Mont Salêve, Chamounix
- Italy: Naples, Como, Milan, Leghorn (Livorno)
- Germany: Ingolstadt, the De Laceys' cottage, Strasbourg, Rhine valley, Cologne
- France: Paris, Lyon, Rhône valley
- England: London, Windsor, Matlock, Lake District
- Holland: Rotterdam
- Scotland: Perth, Edinburgh, Orkneys
- Ireland

Literary context

Gothic literature

Features of Gothic

While many critics have tended to see the Gothic as a loosely defined form, it is nevertheless possible to identify a wide range of features typical of works that fall within the genre. The following list covers the most common, all of which are highly significant in a consideration of *Frankenstein*:

- wild landscapes
- religious settings/concepts
- sudden shifts of emotion
- excess and extremity
- the supernatural and ghostly
- darkness, shadow, decay
- the exotic and oriental
- horror and terror
- isolation and loneliness
- sanity and insanity
- multiple narrators
- absolute power
- the arcane
- the outsider

Shelley employs many of these devices; however, *Frankenstein* is also different from the conventional Gothic world of Radcliffe or Lewis. You need to explore Shelley's use and subversion of Gothic conventions.

The development of Gothic

Gothic first emerged as a recognisable form in the mid- to late eighteenth century. *The Recess* (Lee), *The Old English Baron* (Clara Reeve) and *The Castle of Otranto* (Horace Walpole) date from this period and are generally recognised as the first flourishing of the form. Radcliffe (*The Mysteries of Udolpho*, *The Romance of the Forest* and *The Italian*) and Lewis (*The Monk*) established the classic form, pursuing two contradictory impulses in Gothic — Radcliffe exploring terror, Lewis horror. The form developed in the works of Maturin (*Melmoth the Wanderer*), Hogg (*The Private Memoirs and Confessions of a Justified Sinner*), Godwin (*Caleb Williams*) and Mary Shelley.

The Victorian era saw Gothic fiction from Joseph Sheridan le Fanu (*Uncle Silas*, *The Wyvern Mystery*), Dickens and Elizabeth Gaskell, amongst others. It also spawned a related genre in the sensation novels of Collins, Mrs Henry Wood and Mary Elizabeth Braddon, which brought the terrors of Gothic into the domestic sphere. At the end of the nineteenth century and into the twentieth, new versions of the form proliferated in the decadence of Oscar Wilde (*The Picture of Dorian Gray*), Stevenson (*The Strange Case of Dr Jekyll and Mr Hyde*) and Stoker (*Dracula*), the ghost stories of Henry James and M. R. James, and the adventure novels of Arthur Conan Doyle, Henry Ryder Haggard and Wells. In

Task 15

Identify examples of each of the devices in the novel listed. Explore the comparisons and contrasts that emerge with other Gothic texts you have read.

Taking it Further ▶

Ken Russell's film *Gothic* imagines the house party where the Shelleys, Byron and his physician John Polidori told ghostly tales, leading to the writing of *Frankenstein*. Passer's film *Haunted Summer* deals with similar issues. Watch the films and see what illumination they cast on the novel.

all of these writers, where fear of the outsider in the closing years of Empire is paramount, the way is paved for the more overtly arcane (H. P. Lovecraft) and horrific (Edgar Allan Poe, James Herbert, Stephen King) that has dominated the form over the last century.

Roots of Gothic

The roots of Gothic precede Walpole, Lee and Reeve. Here are some key authors and movements which influenced its rise:

- Elizabethan and Jacobean tragedy (Shakespeare, Cyril Tourneur, John Webster, Thomas Kyd)
- graveyard poetry (Robert Blair, Thomas Parnell, Edward Young)
- Blake
- the Romantics (Wordsworth, Coleridge, Percy Bysshe Shelley, Byron)
- the novel of sentiment (Richardson, Brooke, Henry Mackenzie)
- Milton
- medieval Gothic

Dualisms within Gothic

Gothic thrives on opposition and division. It is a genre that abides on the borders and extremes of experience, and it depends upon uncertainty and violent shifts. The unsettling and the indefinable play a central role in Gothic, and *Frankenstein* with its exploration of moral, social, religious and personal doubt is no exception.

Other literary contexts

Paradise Lost

See pp. 43–44 of this guide for an exploration of the structural similarities between *Paradise Lost* and *Frankenstein*. Close connections also emerge between the central characters of both texts.

Throughout *Frankenstein*, Shelley parallels Victor Frankenstein and the monster with Adam, Satan and God. Both Frankenstein and the monster take on elements of each.

The monster and Adam

Like Adam is the first man, the monster is Frankenstein's first creation. Faced with the prospect of a life spent alone, both are isolated, unfulfilled and in need of a companion. Both knowingly commit acts of

> ### Task **16**
>
> A dichotomy is a sharply defined division, such as light/ dark and good/evil. Think carefully back over the novel. What dichotomies does Shelley employ? What is the impact of her use of such stark divisions?

sin against their creator. As Adam did, the monster enters the world with a mature body, but with an 'unformed' mind, which has to make sense of a totally new world. Like Adam, the monster is banished from 'Eden' — both a beautiful physical place and a place offering the possibility of a loving and meaningful relationship with the creator.

There are also two striking contrasts between Adam and the monster. Unlike Adam, the monster is never allowed the pleasure of a partner, as his companion is destroyed. And for the monster, unlike Adam, there is no promise of a coming saviour to provide hope for the future.

The monster and God

Like God, the monster holds power of life and death over Frankenstein. He also consistently sits in judgement over him. As he reminds Frankenstein: 'I am your master.' As the God of the Old Testament pursues justice against the sinful, even down the generations, so the monster becomes a vengeful, god-like figure watching over Frankenstein's movements with almost omniscient powers. Like God, he forces Frankenstein out of the 'paradise' of his family and marriage.

Top ten *quotation* ❯

The monster and Satan

Satan and the monster both rebel against their creators, although the monster does so with good cause. Like Satan, the monster exacts revenge not directly, but by attacking the thing his creator loves most; Satan attacks the newly created humans and the monster attacks Frankenstein's family.

Both the monster and Satan endure amazing hardship. Satan undertakes his daring journey across Chaos, and the monster lives under the harshest of conditions as he roams Europe. Satan is ejected from heaven by God because of his rebellion, and similarly the monster is thrown out of the heaven of social relations by his creator, Frankenstein.

The monster and Satan are both strangely attractive characters who retain something of our sympathy. Blake famously observed that Milton was 'of the devil's party without knowing it'; Shelley is clearly on the monster's side. We frequently feel sympathy and pity for the monster, even in his evil acts. When he decides on a course of evil instead of good ('Evil thenceforth became my good') he echoes almost exactly Satan's resolution: 'Evil be thou my Good.'

Top ten *quotation* ❯

Frankenstein and Adam

Frankenstein, like the monster and Adam, sins against his creator. As a result, he is banished from a happy relationship with his creator and the natural world. He is also banished from the 'paradise' of his family and marriage with Elizabeth. Through his experiments, he metaphorically eats the forbidden fruit of knowledge. According to Milton and his biblical source, the consequence of sin is death. This does not happen immediately (though mortality does enter the world), but Adam is made to suffer for his sins through the death of his relationship with God; as a result of Frankenstein's 'forbidden' experimentation, death enters the novel, embodied in the monster.

Frankenstein and God

Frankenstein plays God in creating the monster. Unlike God, however, he provides no Garden of Eden for his creation to live in, no care, and provides no moral boundaries for him. He forces the monster from the 'paradise' of society, but unlike God, this is not because of disobedience, it is out of selfishness: the monster's 'original sin' is his ugliness, not a defect in his personality. God recognises Adam's need for a companion and supplies him with Eve, but Frankenstein does not live up to his grudging promise to create a mate for the monster, with disastrous consequences.

Frankenstein and Satan

In seeking to create life, Frankenstein usurps the place of God, as when Satan and his legions seek to displace God in heaven, and both have to pay the penalty — ejection from heaven. Frankenstein loses the ability to pray (his only prayers are of vengeance and destruction) and he falls into despair (represented in part by his increasingly tainted relationship with the beauty of the natural world). In an ironic reversal of roles, the monster becomes his master. Frankenstein recognises the similarities between himself and Satan, observing: 'like the archangel who aspired to omnipotence, I am chained in an eternal hell' (p. 214).

Other characters

Elizabeth, Frankenstein Senior and Clerval also draw characteristics and plot roles from *Paradise Lost*. As a group of angels (Uriel, Raphael and Michael) attempts to protect the innocence of Adam and Eve, so Frankenstein's immediate friends and family try to protect him from the encroaching dangers he faces, and from which he is clearly incapable of protecting himself. Frankenstein Senior warns him to avoid the 'sad trash' in the works of Paracelsus and Albertus Magnus (p. 40). Clerval nurses his friend back to health when he falls ill after the creation of the monster, and also accompanies him, almost like a guardian angel, on his trip to England. Elizabeth, as the 'heavenly' language which Frankenstein repeatedly applies to her suggests, is similarly cast in the role of angel.

The Rime of the Ancient Mariner

Coleridge's great poem (*Lyrical Ballads*, 1798) is another text that influenced Shelley's writing of *Frankenstein*. Its influence began early in her life when Coleridge visited the Godwin household. In the evening, Mary and her siblings hid behind the sofa to hear him recite the poem. Mary's stepmother threatened to send them off to bed, but Coleridge intervened, and they were allowed to stay and listen. Detailed comparisons of plot material, concept, location and imagery can all be found within the poem. A close reading of the poem is therefore recommended.

In the extract from 'I am going to unexplored regions' to 'imaginative of modern poets' (pp. 21–22), Walton immediately establishes the importance of Coleridge's poem and its function in the novel; this soon appears to carry significance and symbolic weight belied by Walton's apparently light-hearted allusion. The seeds of danger are already sown: Walton has a passionate desire for the dangers of the ocean, and he is soon faced by a mad mariner, shackled to his own 'albatross', in the shape of Victor. From the outset we are alert to the importance of allusions to the poem.

Some of these allusions are to plot, others are symbolic:

- voyages to the polar regions
- ghostly and supernatural events
- symbolic burdens (albatross/monster)
- extreme locations
- natural world
- compulsive telling of cautionary tales
- thoughtless actions lead to haunting consequences
- spiritual and physical isolation

Taking it **Further**

Read Coleridge's poem *The Rime of the Ancient Mariner*, which is widely available on the internet and in poetry anthologies.

TopFoto

One of Gustave Doré's wood engravings for Coleridge's *The Rime of the Ancient Mariner*

Frankenstein and the albatross

Like the mariner, Frankenstein is cursed to carry the burden of consequences for his actions. When he promises to create a companion for the monster, he calls it a 'deadly weight yet hanging round my neck, and bowing me to the ground' (p. 157). Later he observes: 'I was cursed

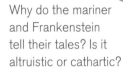

by some devil, and carried about with me my eternal hell' (p. 207). The symbolism of the albatross transposes on to Frankenstein's situation through:

- the monster
- his promise to create a companion for the monster
- his fascination with science
- deaths for which he is (in)directly responsible
- his fear for his family
- his feelings of guilt and isolation

Locations

Both poem and novel make effective use of the polar regions to achieve atmospheres of oppressive strangeness: the barrenness and harshness of the physical location, with its unrelieved whiteness, brilliant displays of light, midnight sun and impenetrable winter nights, create a powerful sense of otherness and danger — suitable homes for bizarre creatures and the supernatural. The isolation of the environment reflects the state of the mariner, the monster, Frankenstein and Walton. It is literally the end of the Earth — a striking contrast to the more civilised environs of England in Coleridge's poem and Switzerland in *Frankenstein*; the hostility, coldness and darkness associated with the poles is symbolic in both texts. Finally, the pole is the place of nemesis, where the Ancient Mariner, Frankenstein, Walton and the monster come face to face with their destinies and the horrible consequences of their actions.

The Prometheus myth

Frankenstein is subtitled *The Modern Prometheus*. Prometheus, whose name means 'forethought', is a divine being, one of the Titans descended from the union of the Sky God with the Earth Mother. In some stories he appears as the creator of the human race, but is always their champion. When humans were denied fire by Zeus, Prometheus stole it for them from heaven. As punishment he was fastened to a cliff in the Caucasus where an eagle daily tore at his liver, which grew back again each night to be torn out again the next day.

Shelley's use of the Prometheus myth is ironic. Frankenstein certainly does not apply 'forethought' to his actions. In fact, his lack of

*Pause for **Thought***

Why do the mariner and Frankenstein tell their tales? Is it altruistic or cathartic?

Task **17**

Victor Frankenstein compares himself directly to the mariner by quoting Coleridge's poem (p. 60):

Like one, on a lonesome road who,
Doth walk in fear and dread,
And, having once turned round, walks on,
And turns no more his head;
Because he knows a frightful fiend
Doth close behind him tread.

In what ways does this help you understand Frankenstein's character?

*Pause for **Thought***

Think about the following characters:

- Elizabeth
- Clerval
- Frankenstein's father
- Justine Moritz
- the monster
- Walton

What 'albatrosses' do they have to bear?

forethought about the being he creates is striking. The comparison of Frankenstein with a divine being, the champion of humankind, is also blackly comic.

Viewed from another perspective, however, parallels with the Prometheus myth add weight and resonance to her moral tale. As the creator and champion of mankind, Prometheus clearly relates to Frankenstein. Similarly, Prometheus's punishment for stealing the fire of the gods relates to the fate of Frankenstein, who also steals from God. As Prometheus's liver is perpetually eaten out on the barren cliff, so Frankenstein is for ever destined to pursue the monster through the wilds of the Earth, and to be destructively torn apart by remorse. The comparisons are instructive, and complete except in one respect: unlike Prometheus, who is eventually freed by Hercules, Frankenstein cannot be released from his torture.

Taking it Further

Why not read Percy Bysshe Shelley's account of the Prometheus myth in his poem *Prometheus Unbound*?

Critical context

The role of literary criticism and literary theory in the study of literature at both AS and A2 is central. AO2 requires critical understanding in analysing the ways in which structure, form and language shape meanings; AO3 looks for understanding informed by interpretations of other readers; and AO4 highlights the contexts in which literary texts are written and understood. Work in all these areas will be enhanced by careful use of critical and theoretical material, which is an essential part of your studies. Criticism and theory, for instance, can be used to understand that:

- the interpretation of literary texts, or the determination of their significance, can depend on the interpretative stance taken by the reader
- literary texts are understood in different ways in different periods, and by different individuals or social groups
- texts do not reflect an external and objective reality, but embody attitudes and values
- there are different ways of looking at texts, based on particular approaches and theories

You need to think carefully about how critical and theoretical material should be used. The emphasis is on your ability to recognise and evaluate the validity of interpretations from a multiplicity of viewpoints. Approaching a text from a single perspective, or prioritising one view at the expense of others, is neither desirable nor helpful. Successful students apply and develop their critical thinking about the set text in the light of a variety of secondary texts.

Criticism and theory are not virtues in their own right, however. Unthinking use of either is at best redundant and at worst prevents you from thinking for yourself. The key to successful application of literary criticism and literary theory is to use it as a basis for argument. There are three basic positions that can be adopted:

- to agree with a critical proposition and to use this to support an argument or part of an argument
- to agree with qualifications — identify clearly what are the areas of agreement, but go on to develop areas of disagreement, qualification, modification or extension of ideas
- to disagree with a proposition, explaining why

All of these stances can be developed by going on to propose alternative critical or theoretical possibilities and evaluating the validity of one critical perspective against another. In other words, you must engage with any criticism or theory you use. Identify clearly the issues raised by the critic, apply these in detail to the set text — which must always remain the primary focus of the response — and then evaluate, giving a personal judgement.

Critical voices

To help make sense of this guidance about using critics, here is a set of worked examples drawing on criticism relating to Gothic fiction, and applying this to *Frankenstein*. It is important here to use critical comment in order to gain a fuller understanding of how Shelley has used the form, and to bear in mind a range of the critical ways in which readers might 'receive' the novel. A secondary aim of this section is, by targeting a number of critical points of view, to provide a basis for thought and discussion when relating *Frankenstein* to your wider reading.

The nature of Gothic

The subversive

> Gothic was the archaic, the pagan, that which was prior to, or resisted the establishment of, civilised values and a well-regulated society. (David Punter, *The Literature of Terror*, 1996)

Pause for Thought

What civilised values and societal establishments does *Frankenstein* challenge? In what ways do you think Shelley is seeking to be subversive?

Note Punter's emphasis upon the 'external' and subversive nature of Gothic, which, he suggests, lies at the very boundaries of the acceptable; hence it is often linked with a historically remote time, or with the religiously suspect (witchcraft, the pagan, non-Protestant religion), the exotic and the foreign. Even where the action of the texts is firmly located in England, setting and events often indicate values and demands that lie outside the bounds of the conventional and the acceptable.

The bizarre and unfamiliar

> **Gothic was chaotic…ornate and convoluted…excess and exaggeration, the product of the wild and uncivilised. (Punter, 1996)**

Gothic is uncontrollable and excessive, bizarre and unfamiliar. It is the continual presence of such elements within Gothic texts that creates its unpredictable and disturbing effects. The atmosphere is often laden with threat and foreboding. The representation of violent and extreme action and emotion, often incompletely explained, and the use of wild locations create a disturbing lack of security. The fictional world of *Frankenstein* makes considerable use of this.

The Gothic borderlands

> **Gothic works, it is often objected, are not fully achieved works: they are fragmentary, inconsistent, jagged…If Gothic works 'do not come out right', this is because they deal in psychological areas which themselves do not come out right, they deal in those structures of the mind which are compounded with repression rather than with the purified material to which realism claims access…And it is here that we come to the crux of the matter: Gothic writers work — consciously or unconsciously — on the fringe of the acceptable, for it is on this borderland that fear resides. In the best works, the two sides of the border are grafted onto each other. (Punter, 1996)**

This quotation identifies the importance of uncertainty and incompleteness within the Gothic world-view. The form represents its contents and concerns; Gothic is not neat and orderly, and therefore the works themselves are frequently neither neat nor orderly. Confusion of action and motive are significant, indicating the very uncertainty and complexity with which the texts engage. Frankenstein is a perfect example of this, proving peculiarly incapable of understanding his own desires and actions. His relations with the wider world, with his family and with the monster he creates, are all problematic and illustrate the importance of confusion and uncertainty. The growing complexity of the relationship between the monster and its creator (who may be taken as the opposite sides of the border referred to in the above quotation) is central to the text, and the distinctions between them become increasingly uncertain as the novel progresses.

Repetition

Frankenstein deals extensively not only with the possibility, but also with the reality of generational repetition. Frankenstein fears the beginnings of a new race of monsters, and therefore disastrously destroys the companion he is creating for the monster. Similarly, the pattern of violent death is visited upon three generations of Frankenstein's family, and Walton, with his fascination for exploration, is a potential new Frankenstein.

Opposites and oppositions

> [The] juxtaposition of the ghastly and the everyday suggests one of the defining characteristics of the Gothic genre, that of the uncanny double, the shadowy world that is the complex underbelly of familiar experience. (Laura Kranzler, Introduction to Elizabeth Gaskell's *Gothic Tales*, 2000)

Kranzler illustrates the importance of opposites and opposition in the Gothic. She suggests the essentially subversive nature of the form and its importance in providing an alternative perception of reality. *Frankenstein* stands in stark contrast to the well-ordered world of the Enlightenment, formality and propriety. The tale operates within the social conventions of the time, but at the same time diverges widely from them.

Blurring the edges

> The Gothic was and remained the dimension of the imperfectly perceived. (Punter, 1996)

Many Gothic narratives, including *Frankenstein*, gain considerable effect from blurring the edges of the narrative. Transitions from narrator to narrator and the varying perspectives they offer of events, along with the uncertainties engendered between the characters of the tale, who frequently parallel one another, are capable of creating in the reader the profound sense of insecurity and unease that underlies the form itself.

The forbidden and its attractions

> It is in its concern with paranoia, with barbarism and with taboo that the vital effort of Gothic fiction resides: these are

the aspects of the terrifying to which the Gothic constantly and hauntedly returns. (Punter, 1996)

Here Punter highlights the essential role of the forbidden and its attraction within the Gothic. *Frankenstein*, like many other Gothic texts, deals with the forbidden and the dangers of pursuing it. This raises questions about the reader's morality and pleasure in reading and enjoying these texts.

Distortion and exaggeration

The Gothic is a distorting lens, a magnifying lens; but the shapes which we see through it have nonetheless a reality which cannot be apprehended in any other way. (Punter, 1996)

Punter's emphasis here is on the importance of distortion and exaggeration in the Gothic. The larger-than-life and the twisted have a vital role to play, he suggests, in assisting the reader to approach certain less pleasant realities of life. In *Frankenstein*, the monster is in a literal sense both distorted in his physical repulsiveness and exaggerated in his size. His grotesqueness, however, reflects on Frankenstein's nature too, revealing his character failings.

Religion

These excluded areas...often retain a strong peripheral or inverted relationship with orthodox religion [and] embrace the practices usually termed occult. In such systems there is much more direct relationship with the invisible realms. (Clive Bloom, *Gothic Horror*, 1998)

Gothic fiction is notable for the frequent appearance of the devil and the devilish. The arcane and the forbidden are staple elements of the works of authors using the Gothic form, such as Aleister Crowley, Peter Ackroyd, Charlotte Dacre and Matthew 'Monk' Lewis. They also have a key role to play in *Frankenstein*; Shelley writes of a world where values are inverted, and where the presentation of religion is at best unorthodox. She makes direct and extensive use of the language of the devilish. The above quotation sheds an interesting light on the role of conventional religion in Gothic, a form which depends for much of its impact on a rejection of the orthodox and the establishment.

Realism and symbolism

Gothic fiction thus finds itself operating between two structural poles. On the one hand, because it rejects the

> account which realism gives of the world, it seeks to
> express truth through the use of other modes and genres
> — poetic prose, the recapture of tragedy, expressionistic
> writing, the revival of legend, the formation of quasi-myths
> — in order to demonstrate that the individual's involve-
> ment with the world is not merely linear but is composed
> of moments with resonances and depths which can only
> be captured through the disruptive power of extensive
> metaphor and symbolism. (Punter, 1996)

Note the importance of symbolism as opposed to realism within
Gothic. Shelley creates a fragile balance between them. The relationship
between the two is essential — a preponderance of either element leads
to an imbalance and a consequent reduction in the effect of the writing
and its ability to instil fear and uncertainty.

Terror and horror

> Terror and Horror are so far opposite, that the first expands
> the soul and awakens the faculties to a higher degree of life;
> the other contracts, freezes and nearly annihilates them.
> I apprehend that neither Shakespeare nor Milton by their
> fictions, nor Mr Burke by his reasoning, anywhere looked
> to positive horror as a source of the sublime, though they
> all agree that terror is a very high one; and where lies the
> great difference between terror and horror, but in uncer-
> tainty and obscurity, that accompany the first, respecting
> the dreaded evil? (Ann Radcliffe, from 'On the Supernatural
> in Poetry', 1816)

The difference between terror and horror is a key distinction as far as
Radcliffe is concerned. She uses it to point to the morally elevating and
uplifting potential of terror, as opposed to the morally and spiritually
enervating impact of horror. Devendra Varma was one of the first critics
to seize on this distinction, characterising the difference between terror
and horror as the difference between 'awful apprehension and sickening
realisation'. Robert Hume has also embraced this distinction, although
in slightly different terms; he argues that the horror novel replaces the
ambiguous physical details of the terror novel with a more disturbing set
of moral and psychological ambiguities.

Robert L. Platzner, while not challenging entirely the difference between
terror and horror, notes where the edges blur. He refers specifically to
the writings of Ann Radcliffe, but the application is more general: 'It
appears that far from never crossing the boundary between terror and

Task 19

Jot down the major
symbols that Shelley
employs and their
effects.

Task 20

To what extent do
you feel Shelley uses
terror and horror?
Find examples of each
and evaluate them in
relation to these critical
views.

horror, Mrs Radcliffe compulsively places her heroine in situations of overwhelming anxiety in which a gradual shift from terror to horror is inescapable.'

Using literary theory

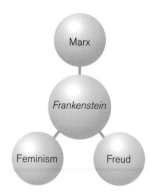

Marx

Frankenstein

Feminism

Freud

Knowledge of a range of theoretical positions will enable you to develop your abilities as an effective reader. Three of the most significant critical movements of the last century have been based on the writings and theories of Sigmund Freud, Karl Marx and feminist theorists. All three approaches cast an interesting light on a reading of *Frankenstein*.

Sigmund Freud (1856–1939)

Sigmund Freud, the psychoanalyst, formulated his theories in a series of books, *The Interpretation of Dreams* being the best known. His work led to many interesting developments in the literary world, including the rise of the psychoanalytic school of literary criticism, which has been highly influential. He is most famous for propounding the concept of the Oedipus complex (an innate sexual attraction to the parent of the opposite gender), the death wish, a focus upon the phallus as symbol and its corollary, penis envy, as well as the formulation of the divisions within the human psyche, which he termed 'id', 'ego' and 'superego'. His ideas and their appearance within Freudian literary criticism relate in detail to the fictional world of *Frankenstein*.

Childhood

Freud's concentration on infancy as the basis for subsequent psychological development is highly significant. The early portion of Shelley's novel focuses on the development of Frankenstein. Considerable significance is attached to the loving home environment within which he grows up, and his father's notable failure to explain clearly to his son the reasons for his disapproval of the young Frankenstein's scientific research. Shelley also presents the reader, in Justine Moritz and Elizabeth Lavenza, with orphaned children. The monster is another significant example of this; Frankenstein, who stands *in loco parentis* to the monster, fails singularly in his parental duties of nurture and affection, leading to the monster's passionate desire for revenge and the devastating events of the novel. Childhood is also significant through Shelley's portrayal of William, the first innocent victim of the monster, and the other children who, even in their innocence, reject the monster early in his life.

Sexuality

Freud believed that sexuality, repressed or otherwise, lies at the root of human behaviour. In *Frankenstein*, considerable emphasis is placed on the idea of 'consummation': Frankenstein speaks of the creation of the monster as the consummation of his dreams, tellingly avoiding sexual intercourse by creating rather than begetting a 'child'; later, fearing the results of a consummated relationship between the monster and any female companion he might create, he makes his fatal decision to renege on his promise to the monster. Frankenstein's marriage to Elizabeth remains strikingly unconsummated, the bizarre consummation of death between the monster and Elizabeth taking the place of marital sexual union. Shelley creates a significant sexual triangle between Frankenstein, the monster and Elizabeth.

Emphasis on the Oedipal relationship between parents and children is at the heart of Freud's theory and also relates significantly to *Frankenstein*. Shortly after he has succeeded in bringing his monster to life, Frankenstein has a nightmare in which the figures of his mother and Elizabeth become entwined. It is significant too that the marriage between Frankenstein and Elizabeth is hastened as the dearest wish of the dead mother, as if she and not the love of the two young people is the driving force in the relationship.

The self

The psychology of the divided self is a further crucial element in Freud's theory. He identifies a three-way division of the human psyche into the 'id' (appetite-driven desires), the 'ego' (conscious sense of 'self' and awareness of others) and the 'superego' (sense of morality, sometimes seen as conscience). In *Frankenstein*, Shelley fascinatingly pursues the development of the monster through various different stages, and Freud's divisions illuminate the reading of the creature's growth towards understanding and revenge. She also significantly presents the divided and deeply flawed nature of Frankenstein through use of the device of the doppelgänger; in this device, the reader can almost perceive an externalisation of the warring elements of the human mind.

The death wish

Freud saw the death wish as a powerful psychological drive, based on a continuing desire to return to the womb. This can be linked to Gothic's frequent use of dark, enclosed spaces. The garret where Frankenstein creates the monster, for example, is like a nightmarish womb. Frankenstein and the monster are locked in a pursuit to the death, and at times both express a wish that their sufferings could be ended by death

The garret where Frankenstein creates the monster...is like a nightmarish womb

(the monster's final desire is for self-destruction, and Frankenstein refers to his own death repeatedly).

Karl Marx (1818–83)

Karl Marx is best known for his great work *Das Kapital*, in which, with Friedrich Engels, he launched an outspoken attack on the capitalist system. His concept of 'historical materialism' has been highly influential in the Marxist school of literary criticism; this school seeks to understand literature as a form of material production that participates in and illuminates the processes of history.

There are many perceived social or political 'messages' within *Frankenstein*. The novel clearly poses questions with regard to the social implications of science; it also delivers forceful messages on social inclusion and exclusion and their potential consequences. The particular historical and sociological period of the writing of the novel can be linked to the key Marxist concept of class struggle. *Frankenstein*, first published in 1818, was written against the backdrop of European revolution; the monster can be seen as a symbol of the destructive forces of social and political revolution.

> ...the monster can be seen as a symbol of the destructive forces of social and political revolution

The reader also needs to consider how plot, characters and settings reflect the concept of class struggle, either by inclusion or by omission. *Frankenstein* gives a symbolic status to both Frankenstein and the monster, allowing for a wide variety of readings in terms of the relationship between the powerful and the powerless. Shelley also makes extensive use of 'wilderness' settings, the harshness of which reflect the harshness of the monster's life and the brutality of the struggle between the creature and the creator. Shelley's use of a wide range of European locations serves to emphasise the universal nature of the dangers signalled within the novel.

A final key concept here is the way that, through class struggle, characters become 'outsider' figures and are alienated from society. The novel is full of such characters. Frankenstein and the monster both become social outcasts and misfits; similarly, the De Laceys, Safie and her father are victims of society's rejection. Justine Moritz and Elizabeth Lavenza are also social 'misfits' in that both are orphans.

Feminism

Feminism is a modern tradition of literary criticism and polemic devoted to the defence of women's writing or of fictional characters against the condescension of a predominantly male literary establishment.

Significantly, one of the earliest proponents of the feminist cause was Mary Wollstonecraft, Mary Shelley's mother. A number of ideas central to the feminist point of view are highly relevant to *Frankenstein*.

The relative silence and passivity of female characters in Gothic texts has been noted by many critics. *Frankenstein* challenges many of the typical perceptions of women in Gothic; the women in the novel are no more helpless in the face of the monster than men; Frankenstein's mother, Elizabeth, Safie and Justine, in particular, are all notable for their strength of character. However, the stereotyping of female characters according to male fantasy is a criticism levelled at *Frankenstein*, in which Safie, Elizabeth and Agatha De Lacey are all presented as types of idealised female beauty and devotion.

The concerns and plight of women are dealt with in a number of ways. Frankenstein clearly perceives Elizabeth almost as a possession and as his by right. The text also highlights the position of women under Islam, through its presentation of Safie. Even though many of the women in the novel are strong characters, they are still largely obliged to live under the protection of males. As a text by a woman addressing the position of women in society, and women under threat, the novel explores the interesting relationship between the female author and her text, begging questions not only of male fantasy, but also of female fantasy. Given the importance of Freudian readings of Gothic texts, the reader also needs to consider the extent to which such issues could be seen as an expression of a female fantasy or wish-fulfilment.

*Pause for **Thought***

Many writers of Gothic fiction have been women. What is there in the nature of Gothic that might explain this? Why would the Gothic appeal as a means of expression for these women?

Working with the text

Meeting the Assessment Objectives

The four key English Literature Assessment Objectives (AOs) describe the different skills you need to show in order to get a good grade. Regardless of what texts or what examination specification you are following, the AOs lie at the heart of your study of English literature at AS and A2; they let you know exactly what the examiners are looking for and provide a helpful framework for your literary studies.

The Assessment Objectives require you to:

- articulate creative, informed and relevant responses to literary texts, using appropriate terminology and concepts, and coherent, accurate written expression **(AO1)**
- demonstrate detailed critical understanding in analysing the ways in which structure, form and language shape meanings in literary texts **(AO2)**
- explore connections and comparisons between different literary texts, informed by interpretations of other readers **(AO3)**
- demonstrate understanding of the significance and influence of the contexts in which literary texts are written and understood **(AO4)**

Try to bear in mind that the AOs are there to support rather than restrict you; don't look at them as encouraging a tick-box approach or a mechanistic, reductive way into the study of literature. Examination questions are written with the AOs in mind, so if you answer them clearly and carefully, you should automatically hit the right targets. If you are devising your own questions for coursework, seek the help of your teacher to ensure that your essay title is carefully worded to liberate the required Assessment Objectives.

Although the Assessment Objectives are common to all the exam boards, each specification varies enormously in the way it meets the requirements. The boards' websites provide useful information, including sections for students, past papers, sample papers and mark schemes.

AQA: **www.aqa.org.uk**
Edexcel: **www.edexcel.com**
OCR: **www.ocr.org.uk**
WJEC: **www.wjec.co.uk**

Remember, though, that your knowledge and understanding of the text still lie at the heart of A-level study, as they always have done. While what constitutes a text may vary according to the specification you are following (e.g. it could be an article, extract, letter, diary, critical essay, review, novel, play or poem), and there may be an emphasis on the different ways in which texts can be interpreted and considered in relation to different contexts, in the end the study of literature starts with, and comes back to, your engagement with the text itself.

Working with AO1

AO1 focuses upon literary and critical insight, organisation of material and clarity of written communication. Examiners are looking for accurate spelling and grammar, and clarity of thought and expression, so say what you want to say, and say it as clearly as you can. Aim for cohesion; individual ideas should be presented clearly, but these also need to connect into a coherent whole, so there is an evident overall sense of a developing argument. Think carefully about your introduction, because your opening paragraph not only sets the agenda for your response but provides the reader with a strong first impression of you — positive or negative. If you are writing a piece for coursework, it may be worth writing this paragraph last, to ensure that it is an accurate introduction to what you have written, and at the very least you should return to it to make sure it has given a clear sense of your assignment. If you are working under exam conditions, this will not be possible, and you should make sure that as your essay progresses you continue to refer back to your planning and introduction as a guide.

Try to use 'appropriate terminology', but don't hide behind fancy critical terms or complicated language that you don't fully understand; 'feature spotting' and merely listing literary terms is a classic banana skin with which all examiners are familiar. In itself, identifying the use of a particular literary feature proves nothing. What all examiners and other readers will want to see is sophisticated understanding of the effects a

writer has achieved through the use of these devices and an exploration of why this is significant. Consequently, your explanation rather than the simple naming of an effect is most important.

Choose your references carefully; copying out great gobbets of a text learnt by heart serves no purpose. In fact, all it underlines is your inability to select apt short quotations to add strength to your argument. Regurgitating chunks of material printed on the examination paper without detailed critical analysis is — for obvious reasons — a reductive exercise; instead try to incorporate brief quotations into your own sentences, weaving them in seamlessly to illustrate your points and develop your argument.

The hallmarks of a well-written essay — whether for coursework or in an exam — include a clear and coherent introduction that orientates the reader, a systematic and logical argument, aptly chosen wider references within the set text and from other sources where appropriate, neatly embedded quotations and a conclusion which consolidates your case.

Working with AO2

In studying a text, you should think about its overall form (novel, sonnet, tragedy, farce, etc.), structure (how it is organised, how its constituent parts connect with each other) and language. In studying a long novel or a play, it might be better to begin with the larger elements of form and structure before considering language, whereas for a poem, analysing aspects of its language (imagery, for example) might be a more appropriate place to start. If 'form is meaning', what are the implications of your chosen writer's decision to select this specific genre? In terms of structure, why does the on-stage action of one play unfold in real time while another spans months or years? In terms of language features, what is most striking about the diction of your text — dialogue, dialect, imagery or symbolism?

In order to discuss language in detail, you will need to quote from the text — but the mere act of quoting is not enough to meet AO2. What is important is what you do with the quotation — how you analyse it and how it illuminates your argument. You will often need to make points about larger elements of the text, such as generic and organisational features which may relate to the whole book, or to chapters, verses, cantos, acts or scenes within it which are usually much too long to quote. For this reason, it is important to learn how to make effective reference to these larger portions of text. Referring to the text means much more than simply mastering the art of the embedded quotation.

Working with AO3

Taking it ▸
Further

Use the suggested
readings in the *Taking it
further* section (pp. 89–92
of this guide) to furnish
yourself with a range of
useful texts for comparison.

AO3 is a double Assessment Objective which asks you to 'explore connections and comparisons' between texts as well as showing your understanding of the views and interpretations of other**s**. You will find it easier to make comparisons and connections between texts (of any kind) if you try to balance them as you write; remember also that connections and comparisons are not only about finding similarities — differences are just as interesting. Above all, consider how the comparison illuminates each text. As with literary devices, it is not just a matter of finding the relationships and connections but of analysing what they show. When writing comparatively, use words and constructions that will help you to link your texts, such as: whereas; on the other hand; while; by contrast; by comparison; as in; differently; similarly; comparably.

To access the second half of AO3 effectively, you need to measure your own interpretation of a text against those of your teacher and other students. Be aware, however, that you should also refer to named critics and quote from them if it seems appropriate, as well as looking at the ideas of major literary theorists. Examiners are interested in your personal and creative views, but also need to see that you have developed an informed response to your text by reading more widely in critical and theoretical views of the text. If your teacher takes a particular critical line, be prepared to challenge and question it. To do this, however, you will need to have looked at a variety of other responses. There is nothing more dispiriting for an examiner than to read a set of scripts from one centre which all say exactly the same thing, so make sure you enable yourself to introduce variety into your writing. Top candidates produce fresh personal responses, so do not merely regurgitate the ideas of others, however famous or insightful their interpretations may be; make sure you always respond critically to what they say.

Of course, your interpretation will be convincing only if it is supported by clear reference to the text, and you will be able to evaluate other readers' ideas only if you test them against the evidence of the text itself. Achieving AO3 requires more than quoting someone else's point of view and saying you agree, although it can be very helpful to use critical views if they push forward an argument of your own and you can offer relevant textual support. Look for other ways of reading texts — from a Marxist, feminist, new historicist, poststructuralist, psychoanalytic, dominant or oppositional point of view — which are more creative and original than merely copying out the ideas of just one person. Try to show an awareness of multiple readings with regard to your chosen text

and an understanding that the meaning of a text is dependent as much upon what the reader brings to it as what the writer left there. Using modal verb phrases such as 'may be seen as', 'might be interpreted as' or 'could be represented as' implies that you are aware that different readers interpret texts in different ways at different times. The key word here is plurality; there is no single meaning, no right answer, and you need to evaluate a range of other ways of making textual meanings as you work towards your own interpretation.

Working with AO4

AO4, with its emphasis on the 'significance and influence' of the 'contexts in which literary texts are written and received', might at first seem less deeply rooted in the text itself, but in fact you are considering and evaluating here the relationship between the text and its contexts. Note the word 'received': this refers to the way interpretation can be influenced by the specific contexts within which the reader is operating; when you are studying a text written many years ago, there is often an immense gulf between its original contemporary context of production and the twenty-first-century context in which you receive it.

To access AO4 successfully you need to think about how contexts of production, reception, literature, culture, biography, geography, society, history, genre and intertextuality can affect texts. Place the text at the heart of the web of contextual factors which you feel have had the most impact upon it; examiners want to see a sense of contextual alertness woven seamlessly into the fabric of your essay, rather than a clumsy bolted-on rehash of a website or your old history notes. Try to convey your awareness of the fact that literary works contain embedded and encoded representations of the cultural, moral, religious, racial and political values of the society from which they emerged, and that over time attitudes and ideas may change until the views they reflect are no longer widely shared. And you are right to think that there must be an overlap between a focus on interpretations (AO3) and a focus on contexts, so don't worry about pigeonholing the AOs here.

Essay planning

This section looks closely at an example essay plan. It is a much longer plan than would be realistic for an examination essay, aiming to give a full coverage, and other approaches could of course be equally valid. The points identified would need to be illustrated with well-chosen examples and quotation from the text.

As well as the sample essays online, essay planning activities are provided in the Downloads at **www.philipallan.co.uk/ literatureguidesonline**.

Example essay plan

Sample question

> **In her 1831 introduction to the novel, Shelley explained how she wanted to 'curdle the blood and quicken the beatings of the heart'. Do you think she achieves her aim? In your answer you should write about:**

- **Gothic elements**
- **the way Shelley tells the story**
- **how different readers might respond to terror throughout the novel**

Possible plan

Gothic elements

Frankenstein is a loner. He frequently and dangerously works alone (e.g. at Ingolstadt and on the lonely and desolate Scottish isle). This leaves him far from help and therefore very vulnerable. This kind of separation from society and assistance is typical of Gothic. Both Frankenstein and the monster appear as outsiders, a dangerous threat to societal stability — again typical of Gothic texts. Shelley uses a vocabulary of evil, death and darkness which is typical of the Gothic genre. The conflict between good and evil is a key device — note how Shelley blurs the distinction, however. Emphasis on revenge is frequently found in Gothic fiction and is central to this novel. Shelley makes use of the vocabulary of dreams and the supernatural (Frankenstein is 'like a restless spectre'). There are sudden and violent shifts of emotion.

Story-telling

Shelley's use of location and darkness create a sense of desolation, fear and suspense throughout. The monster, a threatening presence conjured physically out of Frankenstein's thoughts, heightens tension. Note her extensive use of pathetic fallacy to reflect events described. The natural world is a key device in the novel as a whole. Other features include

extended literary parallels to *The Rime of the Ancient Mariner*, *Paradise Lost* and the Prometheus myth, all of which reflect upon and direct the events and concerns of *Frankenstein*. Shelley makes effective use of the doubling of events — e.g. Frankenstein destroys the monster's companion and dumps her body in the sea, so the monster murders Clerval and does the same; the destruction of Elizabeth links directly to Frankenstein's destruction of the monster's companion; also, like Justine Moritz, Frankenstein finds himself falsely imprisoned for a murder he did not commit.

Readers' responses

Consider the difference between terror and horror, the reasons why they are used and the differing effects they have on the reader; comment on the cumulative effect of events of fear and repulsion through the novel. Some readers may have some sympathy for Frankenstein as he faces a terrible moral dilemma and its aftermath. Others may sympathise with the monster, the victim of a thoughtless and vindictive creator. The terror and horror of the novel may be seen as a moral judgement on Frankenstein.

Essay questions

Make sure you know which Assessment Objectives are examined by your board, and bear these in mind as you prepare your answers. AO1 assesses whether your use of language and your writing skills are appropriate to a student at A-level, and is judged on your entire response. Other important issues relate to your organisation of material and your familiarity with the whole text(s). The other AOs may be assessed more locally within your responses, and need to be carefully planned for.

Responses to critical comment

Sample question

> **'For all its violence and the radical challenges to social order it presents, *Frankenstein* is an extremely moral tale.' How useful and truthful do you find this as a view of the novel?**

Possible approach

- The quotation takes for granted that the novel is both violent and radically challenges the established social order. These are propositions which cannot reasonably be challenged, and so the question hinges

Context

'To make anything very terrible, obscurity seems in general to be necessary. When we know the full extent of any danger, when we can accustom our eyes to it, a great deal of the apprehension vanishes' (Edmund Burke, *A Philosophical Enquiry into the Origin of Our Ideas of the Sublime and Beautiful*, 1757).

Think about this in relation to the essay plan above. How could this be included in answering this question?

on the issue of morality, and whether Shelley's intentions are in fact moral.

- Ample opportunity exists to explore contexts and to meet the requirements of AO4. Establishing what the social order looked like at the time of the novel's composition — the social backdrop of established religious views, scientific exploration, radical politics and Shelley's very personal connection with these are all relevant.

- Narrative technique can be explored in relation to literary convention and the various literary models that Shelley employs — Gothic fiction provides a generic background, and its features can be referred to here, but specific reference to the moral weight of *Paradise Lost* and the Romantic backdrop of *The Rime of the Ancient Mariner* are also relevant. All of these will help address the notion of morality in literature.

- Further issues relating to AO2 come through Shelley's use of language. Explore the language of good and evil — this will be very helpful in establishing the moral compass of the novel, and will help judge of its moral intentions.

- AO3 looks at issues of alternative interpretation, and there is plenty of scope here for discussion. Are Shelley's intentions in fact moral? Consider what lessons (if any) Shelley wishes to teach us through the novel. Does she have a moral or didactic purpose, or is her intention primarily to titillate and entertain with a dangerous, forbidden topic? This was, after all, the original intention behind Byron's famous story-telling competition. The various critical perspectives on Gothic fiction on pp. 67–72 of this guide will provide useful ideas here.

- You should draw a final conclusion, identifying whether you believe entertainment or morality is the intention of the author, or whether you think she strikes a subtle balance of the two.

Comparative questions

Wider reading is an important part of your A-level study. Questions and tasks are likely to require you to compare and contrast *Frankenstein* with another text or texts you have studied. Sometimes this text will be established for you by the requirements of your exam board; sometimes the choice of other text or texts will be up to you.

Sample question

> **'Fear and pleasure, pain and enjoyment are fruitful bedfellows.'**
> **Comment on this view of *Frankenstein* and one other text you have read.**

Possible approach, comparing *Frankenstein* with *Dracula*

- In any comparative essay it is important to make sure you select your texts wisely and that they provide interesting and illuminating comparisons and/or contrasts. You also need to think carefully about your argument. Here, the focus on the pleasure to be gained from discomfort — either for the reader or for the characters — is important. In this case, you may wish to explore the pleasure readers take in reading of others' discomfort, the pleasure some of the characters take in inflicting pain on others, and the pleasure some take in feeling pain.

- For AO2, you could identify trains of language throughout the two novels dealing with both pleasure and pain. How far do these exist as separate from one another, and how far do they impinge on each other?

- AO2 also deals with form and structure, and Shelley and Stoker both employ multiple narratives. How does the relationship between pleasure and pain differ from one character's narrative to another? Explore which characters feel pleasure and which feel pain, which cause pleasure and which inflict pain. How is this reflected within the narrative structures of the books? Do we have multiple accounts of single events that provide unusual insights?

- AO3 allows for the exploration of uncertainty, so feel free to explore the shadowy relationship between pleasure and pain. When he marries Elizabeth, Victor already knows that his pleasure is cloyed by pain. What does this suggest? The monster is seen gloating over Frankenstein as he cradles the dead body of Elizabeth. Is he in fact happy about what he has done? Or does this act of revenge actually cause him profound pain? When Lucy Westenra and Mina Harker fall prey of the Count, how far are they in fact victims and how far willing participants? The Count makes it clear that a meeting with him is always willing.

- AO3 also allows you to explore the similarities between characters across texts. Compare the monster and the Count as inflicters of pain. The monster is clearly innocent when he is first created by Frankenstein, but experience and maltreatment turn him to evil. The pain he inflicts causes him deep pain himself. The Count, on the other hand, is calculating and cold from the start — a sinister and deadly force driving deep into the heartland of Victorian England and vigorously enjoying the fact.

- AO4 is about context. Exploring the issue of violence and pain within Gothic fiction is especially important here. Gothic is often about

> The monster is clearly innocent when he is first created by Frankenstein, but experience and maltreatment turn him to evil

shadowy and unacceptable experience, and this is directly relevant here. At the same time, the whole form is predicated on the idea that we take pleasure reading about this. The relationship between pleasure and pain in these novels points to a dark truth about human beings.

Transformational, recreative and creative writing tasks

Sample task

> **Imagine you are Walton. It is two weeks after the death of Frankenstein and you have safely returned to Archangel. After this lapse of time, what is your response to what has occurred? Write one last letter to your sister. Use Walton's style and language and the epistolary form to create an authentic tone.**

Extract from answer

To Mrs Saville, England.

Archangel, 1st October, 17—

And so my feet stand once again on solid ground, Margaret. We reached Archangel yesterday. The crew stayed no longer than to receive their pay, then broke up and drifted away from the ship just as the ice did, releasing me to make my escape. The ice has gone and the crew, but my memories are not so soon shaken. You read a letter from a different man. Day and night I am troubled — a man who was never troubled in his mind before. I feel the arrogance of certainty will never be mine again. If a creature as noble as the hapless Frankenstein could be so overthrown by too much self-possession, then that is no bad thing. I had rather live the rest of my days in doubt. Ours is an age of discovery, but my days of exploration are done, and I will make haste to return to London. How natural the familiar city will feel to me after the wilds of the frozen north.

For the day and night following the monster's departure from my ship I stood fixed to the aft rail, my eyes fixed on the horizon where the raft of ice and the monster it carried had disappeared. Who steered the ship, I know not. Who gave orders I have no recollection. I suppose it must have been me, but the crew would say never a word to me who had so nearly brought about their destruction. I looked back, expecting every moment to see the flames of his funeral pyre leaping upward, staining the sky in parody of the northern lights, but I saw nothing. Perhaps there was nothing to see. Maybe the monster had not the courage to destroy

his own life, even though it had given him nothing but pain. I suppose there is something in all of us that clings fiercely to life, however cold and unendurable it may seem. I will never again be the man I was. Victor had to die, but I can live.

Student commentary

For this final letter from Walton to his sister, I have drawn on the style of the letters from the frame narrative of the novel. Walton's voice, however, has been modified to reflect the changes that he has undergone as a result of his meetings with Frankenstein and the monster. He is no longer the man he was, as he no longer has unquestioning faith in progress and science, and his arrogance is gone. I have employed some of the images from the end of the novel, such as the breaking ice and the monster's funeral pyre, and have tried to apply these to Walton's own situation as he returns to the solid ground of Archangel. This solid ground is in itself intended to be symbolic. Walton is no longer on the shifting intellectual seas representing his voyage, but on something altogether more reliable. This is intended to demonstrate what he has learnt from Victor's terrible tale — the escape he refers to near the beginning. The contrast between vocabulary of life and death is also significant, a technique that reflects Shelley's own use of contrasts in *Frankenstein*.

Examiner's comments

AO1 — quality of writing

- Flawless spelling, punctuation and grammar.
- Vocabulary appropriate to the character of Walton, and modified to reflect circumstances.
- Creates and sustains an appropriate tone.
- Language picks up on and develops the language of the text.
- Suitable metalanguage in commentary.

AO2 — form, structure and language

- Chosen form replicates one of Shelley's key ways of telling the story.
- Language reflects Walton's troubled state of mind.
- Character of Walton is clearly understood, demonstrating close knowledge of the text, and this knowledge is imaginatively applied.
- Use of appropriate symbolic language.
- Use of ideas from the novel which demonstrates sophisticated understanding of the text.

AO3 — different interpretations

- Provides Walton's interpretation after some reflection of some of the final and overarching events of the novel.

AO4 — contexts

- References, actions and speech are appropriate to the time at which the text is set.
- Brief but clear reference to the scientific and exploratory advances of the eighteenth and nineteenth centuries.

*Pause for **Thought*** ❚❚

Coursework tasks involving creative or transformative writing often require an accompanying critical commentary. What issues is it important to cover in such commentaries?

Top ten quotations

'...now misery has come home, and men appear to me as monsters thirsting for each other's blood.' (p. 95)

1

Elizabeth's observations to Frankenstein upon the death of the innocent Justine Moritz emphasise the importance of the idea of monstrosity, and how the monstrous can lurk in the hearts of men. Her words cut deep into Frankenstein's conscience, and there is considerable dramatic irony here as we are aware, as she is not, of Frankenstein's moral guilt for the deaths of both William and Justine Moritz.

'I feel as if I were walking on the edge of a precipice, towards which thousands are crowding, and endeavouring to plunge me into the abyss.' (p. 96)

2

The imagery Elizabeth employs here of precipices and abysses is typical of Gothic fiction. The image of someone walking along the edge of a cliff serves to emphasise the narrow line between life and death, safety and danger, the acceptable and the unacceptable. Liminal states are important throughout the novel, and this image captures such conditions perfectly. It emphasises the fragility of life and captures a sense of imminent danger.

...the fiend that lurked in my heart. (p. 96)

3

'The fiend' — a term Frankenstein often applies to the monster — here lurks in his heart. This is a rich image — it makes clear how far we are to connect the monster and its actions with Victor Frankenstein's own character. It adds considerable weight to the reading that the monster is an externalisation of Frankenstein's own personality. It shows how evil lurks within the human heart.

4   '**I was benevolent and good; misery made me a fiend. Make me happy, and I shall again be virtuous.' (p. 103)**

The monster appeals to his creator. Although most characters in the novel see him as evil — a judgement based solely on his external appearance — the monster asserts his essential innocence and goodness. It is his maltreatment (nurture), not his innate character (nature), that has led to his evil actions. He rightly points out to Frankenstein his responsibilities as his creator to provide him with the conditions for happiness, so that he can again display his virtuous nature.

5   '**On you it rests, whether I quit forever the neighbourhood of man and lead a harmless life, or become the scourge of your fellow creatures, and the author of your own speedy ruin.' (p. 104)**

The monster lays down a very clear ultimatum for Frankenstein. The monster's future behaviour and actions depend upon Frankenstein's response. The quotation emphasises once more the issue of Frankenstein's responsibility and culpability. Frankenstein cannot, after this warning, claim ignorance of the likely consequences of refusing to do the right thing by his creation.

6   '**Was man, indeed, at once so powerful, so virtuous, and magnificent, yet so vicious and base? He appeared at one time a mere scion of the evil principle, and at another as all that can be conceived as noble and godlike.' (p. 122)**

The monster reflects philosophically on the nature of humanity. He points out the good and evil potential of humans, and is astonished that the same race of beings can display at one moment such extreme virtue and at another such extreme debasement. This is a very useful quotation in exploring the character of Frankenstein and all that he represents.

7   '**I am an unfortunate and deserted creature; I look around, and I have no relation or friend upon earth.' (p. 136)**

The monster emphasises the extent of his isolation. In recognising the reality of his own state, he also formulates the basis of his revenge upon Frankenstein. As this is what Frankenstein has condemned him to, so he will force his creator to experience the same.

8   '**My vices are the children of a forced solitude that I abhor; and my virtues will necessarily arise when I live in communion with an equal.' (p. 150)**

The monster shows his dislike of what he has become, and anticipates how this could change if Frankenstein were to provide him with a companion. His use of the word 'children' in relation to his vices suggests the possibilities of generational repetition — these are sins that will be passed down to posterity. Note he refers to his companion as an equal. It is interesting to consider to what extent Victor ever sees Elizabeth as his equal.

> 'Remember that I have power; you believe yourself miserable, but I can make you so wretched that the light of day will be hateful to you. You are my creator, but I am your master — obey!' (p. 172)

9

This quotation excellently captures the reversal that has been effected in the relationship between the monster and Frankenstein. The weak has become powerful, the servant has become the master. Frankenstein, who set out with grandiose visions of being the progenitor of a new master race, discovers that his maltreatment of his creature has made him the basest of all humans. The monster threatens to make life like a living death for Frankenstein.

> 'Evil thenceforth became my good.' (p. 222)

10

This quotation captures neatly the moral reversal that takes place in the course of the novel.

Taking it further

Wide reading is an essential ingredient in the success of the best candidates. A carefully selected reading of other texts by the authors you are studying, critical works relating to the set text and other texts written within the same genre is invaluable in helping you to understand the context of the text you are working on for examination. As you read, note features shared between the texts, explaining how this enlightens your reading of the set text.

The following list is intended to give a range of reading material for the Gothic genre. Not all are conventionally established Gothic texts; they do, however, draw upon the conventions of Gothic to a significant extent, or play with the reader's knowledge of them.

Fiction

- Ackroyd, P. (2008) *The Casebook of Victor Frankenstein*
- Austen, J. (1818) *Northanger Abbey*
- Beckford, W. (1786) *Vathek*
- Conan Doyle, Sir A. (1922) *Tales of Twilight and the Unseen*
- Dostoevsky, F. (1846) *The Double*
- Gaskell, E. (2000, collected edition) *Gothic Tales*
- Godwin, W. (1794) *Caleb Williams, or Things as They Are*
- James, H. (1898) *The Turn of the Screw*
- Lewis, M. (1796) *The Monk*
- Markovits, B. (2007) *Imposture*
- Radcliffe, A. (1792) *The Romance of the Forest*
- Radcliffe, A. (1794) *The Mysteries of Udolpho*
- Radcliffe, A. (1797) *The Italian*
- Stevenson, R. L. (1886) *The Strange Case of Dr Jekyll and Mr Hyde*
- Stoker, B. (1897) *Dracula*
- Walpole, H. (1764) *The Castle of Otranto*

Poetry

- Coleridge, S. T. (1798) *The Rime of the Ancient Mariner*
- Coleridge, S. T. (1800) *Christabel*
- Keats, J. (1819) *La Belle Dame sans Merci*
- Milton, J. (1667) *Paradise Lost*
- Poe, E. A. (1845) *The Raven*
- Shelley, P. B. (1820) *Prometheus Unbound*

Criticism

- Bloom, C. (ed.) (1998) *Gothic Horror: A Reader's Guide from Poe to King and Beyond*, Macmillan.
- Davenport-Hines, R. (1998) *Gothic: Four Hundred Years of Excess, Horror, Evil and Ruin*, Fourth Estate.
- Gilbert, S. and Gubar, S. (1979) *The Madwoman in the Attic: The Woman Writer and the Nineteenth-Century Literary Imagination*, Yale University Press.

- Haggerty, G. (1989) *Gothic Fiction/Gothic Form*, Pennsylvania State University Press.

- Kilgour, M. (1995) *The Rise of the Gothic Novel*, Routledge.

- Kranzler, L. (2000) Introduction to Elizabeth Gaskell's *Gothic Tales,* Penguin.

- Punter, D. (1996) *The Literature of Terror*, Longman.

- Stevens, D. (2000) *The Gothic Tradition*, Cambridge University Press.

Film and television

- Whale, J. (dir.) (1931) *Frankenstein*. The classic adaptation with Boris Karloff in the role of the monster.

- Whale, J. (dir.) (1935) *The Bride of Frankenstein*. As the title suggests, this imagines that Frankenstein, at the suggestion of another scientist, indeed went through with creating a second monster and explores the consequences.

- Smight, J. (dir.) (1973) *Frankenstein: The True Story*. A variation on Shelley's tale, this version combines adaptation of the fictional tale with a psychological exploration of its genesis, and has a different kind of monster.

- Brooks, M. (dir.) (1975) *Young Frankenstein*. Frankenstein's grandson, after years of living down the family reputation, inherits granddad's castle and repeats the experiments.

- Russell, K. (dir.) (1986) *Gothic*. A fascinating film about the house party at the Villa Diodati where Byron, the Shelleys and Polidori held the legendary ghost story contest that gave rise to *Frankenstein*.

- Passer, I. (dir.) (1988) *Haunted Summer*. Another film dealing with the house party at the Villa Diodati. A very different perspective from Russell's.

- Corman, R. (dir.) (1990) *Frankenstein Unbound*. A time-slip movie in which an ultimate weapon (supposedly safe) proves to have global consequences. The scientist involved in the contemporary plot finds himself transported to Frankenstein's Switzerland, where he meets the fictional scientist.

- Branagh, K. (dir.) (1994) *Mary Shelley's Frankenstein*. The modern classic version, with Branagh both acting and directing. A lurid exploration of Shelley's more subtle tale.

Stage version

- Peake, R. B..(1823) *Presumption*. If you would like to compare a stage adaptation of the novel with any of the film adaptations, R. B. Peake's *Presumption* is available online at **www.rc.umd.edu**. Click on 'Electronic editions', then scroll down and select 'Presumption'.

Images of Frankenstein

- A huge range of images is available by searching for 'Frankenstein' at Google Images.
- Bernie Wrightson's excellent illustrations for the novel can be found on Google Images by searching for Wrightson+Frankenstein.

Useful websites

Care needs to be taken when exploring *Frankenstein* on the web. By the nature of the text, many of the websites you may discover will include offensive and/or explicit materials, so be selective. The following selection of materials provides a useful starting point for reliable and useful sources.

- **www.experiencefestival.com/frankenstein_-_film_adaptations** — articles relating to film adaptations of the novel.
- **www.victorianweb.org** — click 'Before Victoria' then 'Mary Shelley' for a brief summary of modern criticism.
- **http://books.google.co.uk** — Fred Botting's book *Making Monstrous: Frankenstein Criticism and Theory* can be found by searching for Botting+Making Monstrous.
- **www.marywshelley.com** — a variety of useful materials, including a selection of relevant online essays, is available by selecting the drop-down menu 'Essays' and selecting 'Mary Shelley and knowledge'.
- **www.intute.ac.uk** — search for 'Frankenstein' to find some excellent resources.